Courageous and Strong

Courageous
and
Strong
A Survivor's Story
of Hope and Healing

Donna G Robinson

Editing by Berryman Editing Services, www.cayceberryman.com

Author Photographs by Jant Daniels Photography

Book Cover Design by Joel Torres, joel.torres0320@gmail.com.

Scriptures are from the *Holy Bible*, King James Version

Disclaimer: Some names and identifying details have been changed to
protect the privacy of individuals.

I would like to dedicate this book to every crime victim survivor who is still standing strong. And to every victim service provider, who spends their days making our lives worth living.

The National Center for Victims of Crime
www.victimsofcrime.org

VictimConnect
National Hotline for Crime Victims
1.855.4.VICTIM (1.855.484.2846)

National Suicide Prevention Lifeline
1.800.273.TALK (8255) (24/7 hotline)
1.888.628.9454 (Spanish)
1.800.799.4889 (TTY)

About the Author

DONNA G ROBINSON IS A writer and speaker who shares her journey of trauma, support and healing. She was the victim of a violent crime that caused her to experience depression, anxiety, fear and many emotions. She attended counseling and joined a support group in efforts to heal. Now, she enjoys spreading awareness on the effects of trauma and how others can overcome. She launched her first speaking engagement during the National Crime Victims Rights' Week. She initially thought her purpose was to only empower victims but she has been given opportunities to speak before victim service providers, those who work with victims. That platform has allowed her to share her experiences in hopes that those who work with victims can better assist them. She will continue writing and speaking to help others heal.

Donna has many years of experience in disaster relief. She holds a BS in accounting from Southeastern Louisiana University and is a native of Franklinton, La.

For speaking engagements or to contact the author visit:
www.donnagrobinson.com

Acknowledgments

⌒

My parents Lucille & Apostle Willie B Robinson.

My family, extended family, friends, and co-workers.

Baton Rouge General Hospital, East Baton Rouge Parish Sheriff's Department, and East Baton Rouge Parish District Attorney's Office.

My therapist, Jacqueline B. Schott, LCSW, SAP.

Moving into the Light Support Group with facilitators Nicole Gillum, LMSW and Charnel Jackson, LPC.

Jennifer Lacefield and many others at Tarrant County Juvenile Services, Fort Worth, Texas.

And, most of all, to my Lord and Savior Jesus Christ who wrapped His grace and mercy around me and held death back.

Blog Post: "I Survived"

I want to take a moment and thank a few special people in my life . . .

To my sister Jean who I called on the phone immediately after the attack crying and confused because I had no idea I had been stabbed. I couldn't figure out why someone would attack me and then run away. But, I remember you praying for me on the phone while we waited for the police to arrive.

To my sweet nephew Ron who was the first to arrive at the hospital. As I laid there in the ER with tears streaming down my face, you grabbed my hand and held it. You are such a sweetheart! Thanks for the nights you spent with me at my place. They are greatly appreciated.

To my brother Ron, or should I say my over-protective brother, who came to see about me and could have landed in a jail cell looking for my attacker . . . but only God! Thanks for being there for me. I will never forget the kiss you placed on my forehead when you came into the ER.

To my sister-in-law Elisa who came to the hospital and spent the night with me. I don't know what I would have done without you. I don't think I could have stayed in that big room alone! And, oh yeah, remember the Code Red?

To my sister Joyes who called me and texted me when I arrived in ICU and I couldn't reach the phone because I had IVs in both arms. Thanks for worrying about me because that is what you do. I'm glad you were a stay-at-home-mom at the time. I needed those daily phone calls from you to get my mind off me. Thanks for visiting me and cooking at my place. You make the best Red Beans ever!

To my sister Janice who said, "I am glad to hear your voice." I remember those were the first words that came out of your mouth when I first talked to you. I'll never forget. Thanks for your legal expertise and to all of your co-workers at Tarrant County District Attorney's Office who aided me. I don't know what I would have done without having an understanding of the court system. Thanks for the things you did to help me through my healing process . . .for the candles to help relax the tension in my muscles; for taking pictures of me to help me feel good about myself when I had been violated; for the decorating ideas we talked about.

To my brother Tommy, my Sunday morning caller, who prayed for me. Even though you worried and thought that God may take me home that day, thanks for having the faith to believe that He wasn't finished with me yet. Thanks for the phone calls and for your church family who sent prayers my way. I needed every single one of them.

To my parents who went above and beyond for me. Thanks for dragging me down the thermal cup aisle at Walmart two weeks before my incident. That cup helped save my life . . . some of the knife punctures went into the cup instead of me. To my mom who served me breakfast and dinner every day after I got out of the hospital. Watching me like a hawk is what you do best! No heavy lifting, no nothing! For making me eat liver and drink grape juice when my blood count was low—only you can do that. To my dad who prayed for me. You are my covering and my shield. You stood in the gap for me when I couldn't pray for myself. There was so much more that you guys did that I can't tell it all . . . for the nights you came and stayed with me; for the times you prayed over me when I cried because fear was trying to grip me, overtake me, and didn't want to let me go; for asking me every morning how I slept the night before when I had only gotten in four or five hours. Words can't really express how much I truly appreciate the both of you.

To my entire family: parents, brothers, sisters, sister-in-law, brother-in-laws, nephews, and nieces. Thanks for everything you've done. For those who took time off your jobs and drove for miles and hours to be with me during my court hearings. For those who took your kids out of school to come and see me. For the phone calls, texts, cards, and letters . . . I appreciate it all. As a family, we made it through this ordeal. We stuck together and pulled through. We didn't give up even when the defense attorney thought he could wear us out but there is power in numbers and we showed up every single time. I didn't survive alone but we survived together! I love you all so much . . . hugs and kisses!

To every other person who provided comfort to me in some way—visits to the hospital, visits to my house, phone calls, texts, Facebook messages, blog messages, flowers, get well cards, letters of encouragement, financial support, words of comfort, laughter, concerns, and prayers—I THANK YOU! What you did will not go unnoticed. God will reward you greatly.

Table of Contents

Introduction

*Have I not commanded thee? Be strong and
of a good courage; be not afraid, neither be
thou dismayed: for the Lord thy God is with
thee whithersoever thou goest. (Joshua 1:9)*

Somewhere between 6:00 a.m. and 6:15 a.m. on
September 15, 2014, I walked outside my apartment to go
to work and was attacked and stabbed by a fourteen-year-
old juvenile. Without my knowledge, he stalked me. He
targeted me. He didn't rob me or rape me but violently
forced a knife inside my body that left a wound in my liver
almost the length of a writing pen. But this isn't about him.
This is my story of hope and healing. This is my experience
of a journey that started one Monday morning in Baton
Rouge, La.

It only took seconds for my life to change. It took seconds for me to walk into a war zone and be ambushed,

unprepared and unprotected. In the hours and days that followed, I was in a total state of shock. Numb. I couldn't believe that something like this happened to me. I was so confused that I couldn't wrap my mind around it.

In the beginning, I was a fighter. I put on my armor and I went into battle. Every negative emotion that God had created, I was introduced to. But, I wasn't going to allow fear, grief, depression, anger, and anxiety to take me out. I was going to fight to the bitter end and win this thing. But, things got worst. I found myself on a roller-coaster ride. Things got so bad that I grew tired and started having thoughts of suicide. But, things weren't supposed to be this way. This wasn't supposed to be my story. I was the faithful Christian who grew up in church and was born to parents who had been in ministry for over fifty years. I was the person who loved God, obeyed His commands and tried to walk in His ways. But, during this storm, I found myself questioning Him. Amidst of my plea for answers, He said absolutely nothing at all and the silence between us seemed to grow louder and louder.

I won't say that when you read this book you'll find a fairytale ending. Actually, I have no idea how this story will end because I'm still living it. I do know that God is the author of my life and holds the pen in His hand. Whatever He decides to write on the pages, that's who I'll be and that's what I'll do.

I won't say that every day has been easy or that I've overcome every obstacle because I haven't. Each day is a milestone. I wake up every morning hoping to survive and heal a little and at night, I reminisce to see if I reached my goal.

I didn't write this book to teach you how to move mountains or guard your life against tragedy and storms. I don't have the answers for that. I just want to offer you hope and words of encouragement. I want to be a written example of someone who has walked through a storm and survived, who stood in the face of adversity with strength and courage. And, I want to let you know that no matter what you're facing or going through, if I can make it, so can you.

CHAPTER 1

The Attack

⤴

And the Lord said, Simon, Simon, behold,
Satan hath desired to have you, that he may sift
you as wheat: But I have prayed for thee, that
thy faith fail not: and when thou art converted,
strengthen thy brethren. (Luke 22:31-32)

IT WAS A STILL, DARK morning like every other morning
when I left for work. I could hear the tapping of my shoes
as I passed my neighbor's doors and walked down the hall
to the top of the stairs, steadying my cup of hot tea with my
bags on my shoulder and my keys in hand. The back parking lot behind building #3 where I lived was U-shaped and
there were storage garages in the center of it with a light
fixture above each door. As I walked toward my vehicle,
which was about the sixth vehicle in line from the handi-
cap parking space that stood near the bottom of the stairs,
someone came out of the darkness beyond the storage

garages. I had seen him plenty of times before, walking to the bus stop or standing outside the gated complex with the other kids. He appeared to be about twelve years old, but I found out later on that he was fourteen. He walked toward me, dressed in his school uniform with his backpack on. Later, after thinking about it, I remembered that he had been hanging around outside in the mornings for the past several weeks. Sometimes, he would wave at me and I would wave back but this time as he waved, I uttered a "good morning" to him.

I was about two feet away from my truck when he passed me. Suddenly from out of nowhere, he grabbed me from behind, and tried to muzzle my mouth shut. I could feel his fingers pressing against my cheek bones. Instantly my arms flew up in defense and I knocked his hand away from my mouth screaming. He wasn't but about an inch or so taller than me and he struggled to contain me. It was dark but I could feel his arms constantly coming in contact with mine as he stood behind me. Every direction his arms went, whether up or down, I tried to block them to protect myself. Although things were happening so fast, I tried to fight him off as best as I could. My intent was to turn around and face him to find out why he was doing this to me. I wanted to take control of the situation and stop this from happening but I didn't get the chance. Suddenly, I fell face forward to the ground. Then everything stopped almost in slow motion. It was dark and silence was everywhere. I looked up and saw him trotting away. With my face to the ground, I could hear his shoes bumping against the pavement as he ran off. I jumped up and followed him for a few feet, screaming. This time it wasn't a scream for help. It was a scream that came from the pit of my stomach, something I didn't even know existed inside of me. I couldn't stop screaming; I was so angry and afraid. I was afraid that he'd come back and kill me, and angry because he violated me. I was innocent, minding my own business, and I didn't deserve to be treated that way. When he heard it, he looked back, startled, and his escape changed from a mere trot to a full-fledged sprint.

After he ran off, reality set in, and I stopped running and realized that it was dark and I was alone. My nerves started to get the best of me. I was scared and my heart was pounding. I hurried back to my truck and quickly gathered up my things that had fallen to the ground. I climbed inside and locked the doors. I was crying and my hands were shaking so bad that I could hardly put the key into the ignition. I couldn't believe what had just happened. I couldn't believe that someone had come up and attacked me for no reason at all.

He ran toward the south end of the property, so I drove to the north. I parked my vehicle in a parking space where very few cars resided. I backed into one of the spaces, turned on my emergency lights and called the police. I described to the 911 operator what happened to me. At that time, I had no idea that I had been stabbed so I told her that I got attacked. I told her that I was leaving for work and a kid in the apartment complex approached me, waved at me, and then suddenly came up behind me and attacked me. I described to her what he was wearing and that I had seen him plenty of times before. She asked me if he took anything, my purse or wallet, and I told her no. She connected with the Sheriff's Department and said that someone would be on their way.

While waiting for the police to arrive, I called my sister, Jean. I had lived with her in Fort Worth, Texas for eight years prior to relocating back to Baton Rouge nine months ago, and I knew that she would be up getting dressed for work. When she answered the phone, I cried and said I needed her to stay on the phone with me until the police arrived. I told her what happened. I just kept saying over and over that I couldn't understand why someone would attack me. I didn't know that while talking to her on the phone, blood ran down into the seat of my vehicle and on my clothes and in my cup holder. It was still dark outside so I might not have seen it if I looked. But, I remember her praying for me and telling me that everything was going to be alright. I felt so bad for her. I felt bad for dumping such information into her lap for her to deal with without warning so early in the morning. But, she comforted me and I appreciated her for it.

It only took the police about seven to ten minutes to get there. By that time, day started to break. The officer quickly found me on the property and got out of his car. I stepped out and told him what happened in between sobs.

He looked puzzled and asked if I noticed any unusual behavior as if the kid had a mental condition or something, and I told him no. I told him which direction he ran and that he usually catches the bus in the mornings with the other kids. He told me that he didn't see anyone near the gate when he approached it and drove through. He asked for my driver's license to make a report. While he took down my information and called for backup, I decided to try to clean myself up. I had fallen on my right knee and had bruised it pretty bad. My black tights were torn and I saw that my knee was bleeding. The palm of my hands stung because I used them to brace for the fall, and I noticed that my black top that I wore underneath a black-and-white striped jacket was wet and very warm in my stomach area. I assumed I had wasted hot tea on it during the struggle, hot tea that I had just taken out of the microwave right before leaving the apartment. I pulled out a roll of paper towels that I always kept in the back seat of my truck. I took several of them and I wiped down the front of my top several times to try to remove some of the moisture, and shockingly they came away red. Blood red! I was so confused. I quickly pulled up my top and saw a deep cut in my upper abdominal area. I must have made a surprising noise because when I looked up, the officer was watching me. He was standing a few feet away from me next to his car. He asked me what happened and I told him that I didn't know but that I fell. He told me to sit still and asked if I needed him to call for the EMT. Still confused I told him that I didn't know, but he called them anyway. He told me to put pressure on the area until they arrived. As I did, it started to ache. I kept moving around and getting up and again he told me to just sit still. By this time, another officer had arrived. While getting an update from the officer completing the report, he noticed that I was bleeding. A few minutes later, he jumped back in his police truck and headed to the crime scene to look around.

When the EMTs arrived, I probably had changed out paper towels about three or four times with several sheets wrapped around my hand at one time. No matter how hard I pressed against the wounded area, I couldn't stop the bleeding. Blood just kept pouring out like a river. One of the EMTs told me that the laceration looked pretty bad and was very deep. A resident appeared and said he was curious as to why the officers and emergency responders were there, mentioning a screaming woman his girlfriend heard earlier when she took her dog out. I waved at him with my bloody hand to say it was me. He looked at me puzzled trying to figure out what was going on. I was almost bent over because the pains grew. While the officer interviewed him, the EMT placed all the bandages she had put on my wounded area inside a trash bag before I stepped inside the ambulance to leave.

On my way to the hospital, I was so distraught and confused. It was almost as if I was dreaming. Things were spinning out of control so fast, I hardly had time to think. While I tried to figure out why one occurrence had taken place, another one was happening. Not only had someone attacked me just a few minutes ago, but now I lay on a stretcher, bleeding badly. This wasn't the way I was supposed to start my Monday morning. I was supposed to be driving myself to work right about now. But, instead, I was being transported to a hospital in an ambulance.

I started to ache even more. I had sharp pains that started to grow and there was a stinging feeling I couldn't get rid of. My muscles all over my body tensed up and I tried to take deep breaths to relax and ease the pain, but it didn't help. The bumps in the road and the sudden turns were making it worse. I was irritated because I continued to put pressure on the wound with one hand while an IV hung in my other arm. And, because the head of the stretcher was elevated up, it added more pressure to my muscles in my abdomen.

With my one free hand, I called my sister and told her that I found a cut and I was bleeding pretty badly and was being taken to the hospital. She asked me where it was, and I told her. I could hear in her voice that she knew what had happened. I had been stabbed. I told her not to call my parents until I found out what was really going on. They both had hypertension, and I didn't want anyone else admitted into a hospital overwhelmed about me. She promised that she would not but would call the rest of the family to let them know what was going on.

CHAPTER 2

Broken

⤜

The righteous cry, and the Lord heareth,
and delivereth them out of all their troubles.
The Lord is nigh unto them that are of
a broken heart; and saveth such as be of
a contrite spirit. (Psalm 34:17-18)

I don't know why this happened to me. I tried to be the best that I could be in the workplace and in my community. I never thought my life would be broken into tiny little pieces where I can't see my beginning from my end. Everything in my life has been shaken. Sometimes I don't know who I am. Sometimes I wake up and sometimes I lay down with tears streaming down my face searching for answers for the many questions I have inside.

See like you, I once was free. I was free to come and go as I pleased until one Monday morning. Not long ago I was attacked and I became a victim. And before the sun set, even though I was living and breathing inside a hospital bed in the

Intensive Care Unit, a part of my soul died. A part of me was taken away and I don't know why. I think about my life and how much freedom existed before I stepped outside my front door that morning carrying my pastel-color bag with a cup of hot green tea inside my purple thermal cup. I think about how I was whole and in one piece free to do what I wanted to do, go where I wanted to go and be who I wanted to be. But the enemy had a plan to destroy me. Apparently, I must be a threat to him and his army. To use another human being to attack me causes me to believe that he is fearful of the power that lies within me. He is afraid, afraid that I will fulfill my purpose in life, afraid that I will be a light in his dark world.

Blog Post: "Walk on Water"

BECAUSE THE EMTs REPORTED THE incident, medical staff stood outside the ER entrance of the hospital waiting for me. When one of the nurses asked me why was I there and I told her I was attacked, they went to work on me immediately. They wheeled me into a room and for a moment, I wondered where the TV cameras, the director, and the actors were because I felt like I was in a movie of some kind. I didn't know that the scenes you see on TV could potentially be what you experience in real life. This was my first time ever being admitted into a hospital, and I had no idea what to expect but I guess because I was a trauma patient; they took things very seriously.

They lifted me from the stretcher onto a bed. While one cut my clothes off, another was trying to find all the stab wounds by tracing my body from head to toe, while others were cleaning the blood off my hands, sticking an IV into my other arm, and checking my blood pressure all at the same time while asking me questions about my medical history. Medical terminology spewed out of their mouths and flew all over the room. They were checking for everything. As the nurse traced my body, I started to get even more upset when she'd discover an injury and call it out. I had no idea I had that many injuries. Tears poured down my face as I tried to make sense of it all. Things were spinning faster and faster out of control. Too much was going on and I was absorbing so much information about my injured body at one time. I guess to keep me calm, they started asking me questions about what happened and where. As I explained, one of the nurses said she had spent the day before at my complex with some friends watching a football game. They all couldn't believe that something like this could have happened in such a quiet, gated community.

When it was all said and done, I had a diagonal cut on my neck from the bottom left corner that made its way up to my right ear, a small stab wound between my armpit and my left breast, and a laceration in my upper abdomen area.

After everyone played their part, a doctor came over and looked at my injuries. He then told me that they were sending in a surgeon to determine if I needed to have surgery. They wheeled me into another room as I waited. They wrapped a bandage around my abdomen to keep the bleeding down but as my muscles moved, I could still feel gulps of blood spill out. As I lay there, I didn't know what to think or believe. All I could do was cry. I had no idea what in the world had just happened. I couldn't even focus on the fact that I may have to have surgery because I was trying to figure out why someone would do this to me. I was so confused. I felt so vulnerable and exposed and violated all at the same time. I had been robbed of my innocence and I was broken. It was as if I was a piece of glass and someone had taken a hammer and shattered me into tiny little pieces.

A few minutes later, a nurse came in to take some blood. I had always been borderline anemic and with losing so much blood that morning, she fought a battle to draw from my arm. She told me that the police officer had arrived at the ER and wanted to know the severity of my injuries. She told me that the word had gotten out around the hospital that a trauma victim had arrived and everybody was talking about it because that hospital rarely served trauma patients. In between my tears I teased her, trying to bring some humor into my day. I said that I try to be as quiet as I possibly can and sometimes those who are the quietest make the loudest noise. She laughed at me as she gathered her things and walked out of the room.

I texted my boss at work to let him know that I wasn't going to make it to work that day and possibly for many more. I also texted my family and gave them an update. Knowing that I may have to have surgery, I asked if anyone had contacted my parents because I felt like they needed to know what was going on now.

After things had settled down a little, I lay there, left to my thoughts. Every time I thought about it, tears streamed down my face. All I wanted to know was why. Why would someone do this to me? What had I done to deserve it? I didn't even know that kid. Had I offended him in some way and he wanted to retaliate? It wasn't like I did something to him the day before because it was a Monday morning, the start of a brand new week, and I had spent my weekend doing my own thing. On Friday evening, I had gone to the mall and gotten my hair trimmed, on Saturday I cooked and hung out at home, and on Sunday I visited my parents and attended church with them. It was such a mystery to me because he had every opportunity to steal from me, demand money, or even take my vehicle, and he did none of those things. Why? What was his motive or reasoning behind attacking me and stabbing me? As I lay there thinking, the door swung open and my nephew, Ron, walked in. He was a student studying at Louisiana State University and lived in an apartment not too far away. He said his mom called and told him that he needed to get to the hospital right away because I had been attacked.

I was so glad to see him walk through that door. It was a breath of fresh air and it felt like my entire family had stepped inside with just his presence. I tried to distract my thoughts by asking him questions about school and work, but he wasn't much of a talker in that moment, seeing that I was so upset and not really knowing what to say. Sometimes, we sat in silence while my thoughts rambled on. There was so much going on inside my head that non-stop tears would fall again and again. Once, he reached over and grabbed my hand. He just held it. He had no idea what that meant to me.

When the surgeon walked in, he introduced himself and we talked for a moment about the incident. He told me that they were going to transport me to have a CT scan performed to see what was damaged. They pushed me down a hall into an elevator and took me to another floor. When I arrived, they lifted me from my bed onto a table to start the procedure. As I followed their directions and lifted my hands above my head so that they could take pictures, I could feel more blood spewing out of my body every time my muscles moved. More tears ran down my face trying to understand all of this. How did I end up here? I was supposed to be at work not lying under a CT scanner having pictures taken of my body. None of this made sense to me. After getting the results back, the doctor informed me that I had some internal bleeding and that there was a laceration in my liver about the length of a writing pen. He said that because the liver heals itself, no surgery was needed. He would stitch me up and allow it to heal, but they were going to place me in ICU and monitor me to determine if I needed a blood transfusion.

Before the surgeon closed up my wounds and I was taken up to ICU, my brother, Ron, arrived. He came in and kissed my forehead, though he looked worried. We talked for a while and I told him what happened. He said that my parents were on their way but I found out after overhearing a phone conversation he had with my sister, Joyes, that they weren't going to make it. My dad got too upset and couldn't drive to the city. Both my parents, in their seventies, take medication for hypertension. My dad wasn't at home that morning when my sister called my mom to give her the news; he was at physical therapy. When he got back, Mom asked if he had taken his medicine and he said no. She asked him to take it because she had something to tell him. He was so anxious nearly forcing her to tell him what was going on that the medication hadn't gone into effect when she gave him the news and his blood pressure rose really high. He got really nervous and upset. Because my mom doesn't drive in the city, they decided to stay home. They had intentions of coming later on but only if my dad felt better. If not, they said they'd come the next day. I was glad that they stayed and didn't drive the hour and a half to see me because my emotions could have possibly made things a lot worse.

As my brother and I sat and talked, a detective from the Sheriff's Department walked in and introduced himself. He handed me his business card and asked me what happened. I started from the very beginning, trying to remember every little detail, but he never pulled out a pen or notepad to write anything down. He just stood there.

The only question he asked was if my attacker robbed me or took anything from me and I said no. He never asked for a detailed description, what time it happened, or anything. Then, I remember him saying, "Because he didn't kill you, I don't know what to charge him with. Clearly, we can see that you're still alive." Then he mentioned something about trying to figure out who would get the case.

My brother and I just sat there and stared at him. We weren't expecting something like that to come out of his mouth. I think we were both a little baffled. I thought, I don't work for the Sheriff's Department, I have no idea what your job duties are. All I know is that someone tried to kill me and I think the law enforcement officer who has been assigned to this case should do something about it. And, who says something like that to a crime victim lying in a hospital bed about to be taken up to ICU anyway? Shouldn't law enforcement have some form of empathy for those they serve? I gather that all of them do not.

He didn't seem to be bothered that someone tried to take my life but was less concerned because they didn't. He was more concerned with confirming if this was going to be his case or if he could shove it off on someone else I guess. He was very inconsiderate and showed no compassion at all. Before he walked out the door, he said that he was going to talk to the surgeon and he would be in touch. Later on, I asked the surgeon if someone from the Sheriff's Department came and talked to him when I was in the ER and he told me no. I never heard from the detective again.

CHAPTER 3

Angels

~

For he shall give his angels charge over thee,
to keep thee in all thy ways. (Psalm 91:11)

WHEN I TRANSFERRED TO THE ICU, I met my nurse. Her station was right outside my door and there was a window next to it so she could monitor me from outside. At times, I was still overwhelmed with emotions, and I noticed that whenever I'd get upset, she'd come in and ask if I needed anything. I would always shake my head and tell her no. A little later, she came in and we started talking and somehow ended up having a conversation about our faiths. She was a Christian. She told me that she didn't work in the ICU but was asked to work in there that day. She also worked with my surgeon, who she said was one of the best doctors at the hospital. At that moment, I knew she was God-sent. I knew they both were God-sent. Although this terrible thing had happened to me, it felt like God was still working on my behalf. He was interceding for me through-out this ordeal and was sending special angels out to take care of me. I knew He had placed her there just for me to give me a comforting word, and that is exactly what she did. I asked her to pray for me and she took my hand and led me in prayer. As she prayed, I felt a connection between us because she too was a woman of faith. We were from the same faith family and I knew that her prayers would reach heaven and be answered. I kept thanking her over and over again as she went about her day and she just kept saying "It's not anything I've done. This is all God's doing."

Four hours after the detective walked out of the ER, a lieutenant entered my room. He introduced himself and said he was taking over the case and we started to talk. I explained to him in detail what happened as he took down notes. I tried to remember everything I could. I tried to give him a good description of my attacker, what he was wearing, his height, everything. A few minutes later, the lieutenant's phone rang and I could hear him trying to console someone on the other end. I found out that it was his boss who was upset because apparently the other detective shoved the case off on his department and he didn't like it very much. I explained to the lieutenant what the detective said to me earlier and how I felt. Although he didn't comment, I could tell from the expression on his face that he wasn't too pleased with how that was handled.

The lieutenant stayed around for a few hours and I got very comfortable with him. I appreciated him because he seemed to care and was interested in what I had to say. With having lost four hours of investigation time, I was afraid that they weren't going to be able to arrest my attacker that day. I knew he needed to be put away before he hurt someone else, especially if he had killing on his mind. I wanted to do whatever I could to stop that from happening. It bothered me to know that someone who tried to take my life was possibly at school hanging out with innocent kids and teachers and they had no clue as to what was going on inside his head or what he had done to me. And, to lose four hours of investigation time, to me, was crucial. I think that is what really made me upset with the unbothered detective.

I was so determined to get him off the streets that I started asking the lieutenant questions, trying to help him solve the case. He finally told me to let him handle the investigation while I focused on getting better. As stubborn as I was, I put my two cents in anyway. I finally told him that apparently, they don't solve cases as fast as the TV show CSI. I said that CSI solves cases within forty-five minutes of TV time or less. He couldn't help but laugh at me. He told me that if he didn't take his time and do it right, my attacker could easily walk and that wasn't a chance he, or I, was willing to take.

He called a forensic photographer to come by and take some pictures of my injuries for evidence. Because my attacker had touched the perimeters around my mouth, my neck, and my clothes during the struggle, the lieutenant also anticipated possibly getting some of his DNA. He asked if I still had my clothes and I said yes. When the nurses stripped them off, they stuffed them inside of a bag including my jacket, skirt, and shoes, and gave them to me. I pointed to the chair standing next to me and told the lieutenant they were sitting beside my purse. He had the forensic photographer to take my jacket and bag it. He also had him to swab my mouth to compare my DNA with possibly that of my attacker's, and they tried to get evidence from my neck assuming that some was still there. I really didn't think that they would find any evidence around my mouth or on my neck because I had cried so much that the tears had probably washed it all away but I remained hopeful anyway.

Even though both the photographer and the lieutenant worked for the Sheriff's Department, fear still crept up inside me when they got ready to take pictures of my body. My brother had stepped out to get some lunch and my nurse was sitting at her station outside my room. I didn't know if she knew what they were getting ready to do so I desperately waved for her to come inside. But, she assured me that she knew and told me not to worry that she was going to be right beside me. Even though I could see their shiny badges, my level of trust was nonexistent. My defense mechanisms were to protect myself in any way possible and the best I could do lying in an ICU bed hooked up to machines was to have my nurse in there with me. I couldn't afford to let anyone else hurt me. It was an uncomfortable feeling. My body had already been violated and brutalized, and the only thing I wanted to do was protect and cover it. A wave of relief came over me when the nurse told them that the doctor only gave them permission to take pictures of my visible wounds, the neck, and the small laceration, but he wasn't going to remove the bandages around my abdomen area. Yes, I wanted them to have as much evidence as possible for the case but not having my body exposed was a risk I was willing to take.

That Monday was probably the worst day of my life, but I thanked God for bringing angels to make it all better. From my doctor to my nurse to the lieutenant and everyone else who played a helpful part, they all seemed to care. They all seemed to have a heart for people just like the God I served. Without a doubt, I knew that they were specifically hand-picked by God and assigned to take care of me that day. I knew He had placed them along my path to make my horrific day flow just a little bit smoother.

I thank God for angels.

CHAPTER 4

Into the Night

‿౭

*Be careful for nothing; but in everything by
prayer and supplication with thanksgiving
let your requests be made known unto God.
And the peace of God, which passeth all
understanding, shall keep your hearts and minds
through Christ Jesus. (Philippians 4:6-7)*

LATER THAT EVENING, MY NEPHEW came back after attending classes to sit with his dad and me. When visiting hours were over, they left. I was comfortable being alone, but I didn't get much sleep that night. My nurse left that evening and another one came on board. I didn't like the changing of the shifts because so much had changed in my life that day that I needed something to remain consistent. When she left, I felt like I was losing something—like I had almost lost my life. When the evening nurse walked in and we started to talk about my day, I remember her telling me that God had a purpose for my life because I was still here. I could feel her warmth and kindness which made me feel a little better.

I tried to find something to watch on TV to keep my mind occupied, but every channel I turned to and almost every TV show seemed to have some form of violence in it. Even shows that were usually my favorite now bothered me. It was such a weird feeling. It felt like I had been locked up in darkness and now I was exposed to such a bright light that my sensitivity level was heightened. I just wanted to watch something soothing that would keep me calm on the inside. I tried watching a sitcom but even that didn't work. I just wasn't in the mood for humor. It contradicted with how I was feeling and it made me uncomfortable. I tried to find a Christian station to watch, but nothing was available so I just kept it on the Home Shopping Network for noise so I didn't have to think too much. The more I could block the day out of my mind, the better I thought I felt.

I kept waking up throughout the night. Sometimes, it was because the nurses were coming in to take blood from me, and other times it was because I just couldn't sleep. Something about nighttime made me feel uncomfortable. It represented rest, and resting caused me to think, and that was something I really didn't want to do. I didn't want to think about what happened and how I ended up in the ICU. I just wanted the night to be over. I just wanted noise, people, distractions, and conversations to occupy my mind and push everything else into a back corner.

The next morning, my prayer partner nurse returned, but I didn't get to spend much time with her because they moved me out of the ICU. When my doctor came by to check on me and to see how I was doing, he told me they were going to move me sometime that morning and could possibly let me go home that day or the next. As he talked, I thought more about the attack and the kid. The thought of me being released without that kid being arrested didn't sit well with me. I felt anxious. Both my attacker and I could not walk around free, out on the streets, at the same time. Something had to be done.

The day before, the lieutenant waited around for my doctor to make his afternoon rounds so he could interview him about my injuries, but he didn't get the chance. My nurse told me that it had always been a big conflict at the hospital between the police and the doctors. The police want the doctors to take the time to complete an interview with them and the doctors always complained they never have time. So, I asked my doctor if he didn't mind me calling the lieutenant so that he could talk with him on the phone. Being the good doctor that he was, he was willing to take a few minutes to speak with him and he did. I was so thankful for his willingness to cooperate because under any circumstances, I didn't want anything to fall through the cracks with this case. I wanted my doctor's description of my injuries to weigh heavily on the fact that this kid tried to kill me. This wasn't a joke of some kind; he came prepared to take my life.

While the lieutenant waited for the doctor the day before, he made a promise to me that he was going to pick up my attacker the next morning, but when I spoke with him after my doctor handed me back my cell phone, he hadn't arrested him. He said that there was conflicting information and he needed to make sure he was arresting the right suspect. He said he went over to the complex, parked, and watched him get on the bus. I was highly upset. How could they allow this individual to go to school yet another day? What was I going to have to do to get something done? I didn't feel good about it, but this case was in the hands of the only officer I had come in contact with that I had confidence in because the detective that I met the day before didn't seem to have any compassion for victims at all. It seemed his compassion only was given to those that had lost their lives and were dead. I wanted things to move quickly but the lieutenant was trying to play it safe with no mistakes in sight. I understood where he was coming from, but it still bothered me and I didn't like it.

Just before they wheeled me out to take me to another room, my sister-in-law Elisa walked in. She had her bags in hand and told me that she came to spend the night with me. The room I was assigned to was a couple of floors down and was tucked away at the end of a hallway past the nurse's station. I was thankful that she decided to come and stay with me because it was one of the biggest hospital rooms I had ever seen. It was so big that at least three or four beds could easily fit inside. Being alone in there, I probably wouldn't have gotten any rest that night. Things had dramatically changed for me and only small confined areas started to make me feel safe.

CHAPTER 5

Distractions

⟶⟵

And it shall come to pass, that before they
call, I will answer; and while they are yet
speaking, I will hear. (Isaiah 65:24)

THE DAY FLOWED SMOOTHLY. ELISA and I spent much of the day talking. Her sister-in-law had gone into labor that morning and Elisa was excited about the new baby. Her family contemplated how soon her sister-in-law would deliver because even though this was her third child, she was known for being in labor for just a little while before delivering. Sure enough, Elisa got the news that her sister-in-law had a baby boy and literally held her legs together to keep the baby from coming out in the car on their way to the hospital.

I had quite a few visitors who came by that day to see me and keep me company. A previous boss and a co-worker from my job came by on their lunch break, and my cousin, who worked at the hospital, dropped by again to check on me. She had also come by the day before while I was waiting to meet the surgeon. I was surprised to see her because I had no idea that she worked there. She said the family was worried and some had gotten the news that my injuries were a lot worse than was said. It's kind of like the game that the kids play in school when the teacher whispers something into one kid's ear and by the time it gets to the end of the row, it's a totally different story. I was glad that she came to check on me, though, to let everybody know that I was still living and breathing, and I wasn't fighting for my life like some thought.

I was all smiles when my parents showed up and walked through the door after lunch. I was glad to get their hugs and kisses. My mom said they would have been there earlier but they had a flat just outside of town and had to go back into town to buy a new tire and have it put on the car. Since Elisa was going to spend the night with me, they stayed late into the evening and then went back home.

The lieutenant stopped by early in the afternoon. He told me on the phone that morning that he was coming by with a photo lineup for me to identify my attacker. He wanted to make sure that I picked out the right suspect. He gave me about eight headshot photos to look through. They were actually photo ID pictures from the kid's school. The faces of the eight boys nearly covered the entire photo and I was nervous about looking my attacker in the face for the first time. Even if it was a photo, I still felt very anxious. I sat up in the bed with my sweaty palms scrutinizing one photo at a time. To make sure I had the right one, I looked at all the photos twice before I pulled out the one I knew was of him and handed it to the lieutenant.

"That's him," I said. I knew I picked out the right one because I remembered his narrow, skinny face. I almost didn't want to look at him too long, afraid it would bring back horrible memories. I didn't want anything to trigger that moment in time. However, I did take a minute to search his eyes and try to figure out why he would do such a terrible thing. I wanted answers as to why he had chosen me, why he wanted to break my spirit and violate me, but I found absolutely nothing. All my questions were still unanswered.

The lieutenant nodded his head and said he was going to make his arrest. I was thankful to hear that, but I didn't know how the hearing before a judge would go once he was arrested. No one could be certain that the judge would hold him until he was sentenced. The lieutenant said depending on the judge's ruling, they could allow him to bond out. That really didn't make me feel any safer. If that was the conclusion, I knew the judicial system was not going to work in my favor and I didn't like that at all.

My friend, Marcella, came by to see me after she got off work. She was a breath of fresh air after having to deal with a photo lineup and the possibility of the judicial system tactics. The day before, she texted me a little before lunch to check on me and see why I wasn't at work. She thought I'd just played hooky and taken a day off but when I told her what happened, she immediately came to the ER. When she got there, they were getting ready to wheel me up to the ICU so she told me that she was going to come back the next day.

When she walked in the door, she handed me several magazines and word search puzzles. She told me that I was going to need something to do while recovering. She had no idea how much those word search puzzles helped me during those long, dark nights in the weeks that followed. When I couldn't sleep, I'd grab one to occupy my mind, while waiting for my eyes to get heavy enough to fall back asleep. Sometimes, I'd complete about three, four or five of them in one night until I became sleepy enough to lie down and try to rest again.

CHAPTER 6

My Worth

*For his anger endureth but a moment; in his
favour is life: weeping may endure for a night,
but joy cometh in the morning. (Psalm 30:5)*

THE NEXT DAY, I WAS told that I was leaving the hospital
but I had to have another CT scan done before my doctor
would release me. This time, when I got ready to take the
test, I was able to climb up on the table myself rather than
be lifted from my hospital bed. With IVs in both arms, the
hardest part was lifting my hands above my head so they
could take pictures to see if I still had internal bleeding. I
was glad for the progress of getting around even though I
was transported there in a wheelchair. I prayed hard that
the test results would come back good and hoped they
wouldn't find anything else wrong.

When I got back to my room, as promised, I got a call
from the lieutenant saying he had arrested my attacker

yesterday afternoon. He said that he charged him with attempted first-degree murder. He was booked and spent the night in jail at the juvenile detention center. At that time, the lieutenant was in court waiting to go before the judge and would follow up with me regarding the results.

A little later, I got a call from a Victim Assistant Coordinator who worked for the district attorney. She told me that my attacker had gone before a judge and was released without bond, and they reduced his charges to battery charges. She explained that in juvenile cases, they don't take things as seriously and I needed to be aware of that. She said I didn't need to have my expectations too high. I questioned her about the charges. I was appalled. I couldn't believe my ears. He tried to kill me and the charges were reduced to battery. She said in the juvenile court system, battery charges weighed as much as attempted murder charges, but I just didn't believe her. There was no way I believed that. I felt numb hearing those words come out of her mouth. Here I was, a law-abiding citizen who followed the rules, paid my taxes, and tried to contribute something to society, yet I felt rejected by a judicial system that let me down. Whose side were they on? I really didn't care if he was under the age of eighteen, he was a threat to society and that should not have been taken lightly. It was as if I was another random person that caused myself to be put in harm's way. As if I inflicted this pain upon myself. I couldn't believe that they allowed him to walk without even setting a bond and paying a penny. Was I worth absolutely nothing? I guess the trauma he caused me didn't mean anything to them. I just didn't understand it and I was irritated.

My parents picked me up at the hospital and took me over to my apartment. It felt weird pulling into the gates at the complex. I wasn't ready to revisit the memories embedded in my mind that occurred just a few days prior. At that moment, I had so much going on and so many thoughts running through my mind that it really didn't affect me at the time.

I stopped by the managing office on my way and spoke with the manager and the assistant manager. She called me the day before and talked. She told me that the police had been in contact with them and they were fully cooperating. She told me that they were in the process of evicting the guardians my attacker lived with. Apparently, he and his brother had relocated to Louisiana and were staying with some adult cousins. I told her I got a call from the DA's office and my attacker had been released, so he'd be back at the complex that day. Their eyes grew big and they looked worried. I was so frustrated and aggravated that I didn't really care because I could sense that everybody was trying to tiptoe around the fact that I had been attacked and nobody wanted to help me or take some responsibility for it. Maybe it was just me or maybe it was my emotions getting the best of me, but I wanted someone to act like this was important. I could tell that they were trying to cover their own bases in every way possible. So much so, that they weren't even willing to tell the other tenants in the complex what happened and to be aware that a criminal act had taken place on the property because when I asked her about that, she told me she didn't know what they were going to do. There is no way that I could sleep at night knowing that other tenants especially women had not been warned that an individual living in the complex had been attacked. Mind you, it was going to take several days before the eviction process was complete so he'd still live there for another week or two. She tried to explain to me how the eviction process worked, but I really didn't care. All I knew was that I wouldn't be staying there for some time because I was going to my parent's house, and I needed a phone call from them telling me that he was gone and was never coming back. I didn't care what they had to do to make that happen. I was becoming very defensive. It was as if everything was my fault when I was the victim in all of this. The manager tried to comfort me by saying that I could leave my truck parked outside her apartment until I returned, and she'd watch it for me. Ironically, I had parked my vehicle in front of her apartment while I waited for the police to arrive. The morning of the incident, she looked out her window and saw the police cars surrounding my truck. She said when she ran outside to see what was going on, I had already been taken away by the ambulance. She also promised me a reserved parking space outside my front door. When she told me the cost of it, I gave her a look that said I was not paying for anything. Goodness, I had been through enough already. When you're interested in renting an apartment, they give you all the highlights of how wonderful and safe and lighted the property is and how their courtesy officers patrol the area, but when something happens, everybody throws their hands up and says nothing at all. I didn't even know if I'd have enough money to pay my monthly bills being that I had incurred all these extra expenses including medical bills. When she saw the look on my face, she shook her head and said they'd give it to me for free.

As we drove to my apartment, she walked down and called the police officer, who lived in the building across from me, over to introduce himself. I thought it was a little late for that. He was one of the courtesy officers on the property and I never saw him patrolling the complex—he or any of the others she said lived there. I was beginning to get the feeling that everyone was out for themselves, and I was the villain in all of this.

My mom wouldn't allow me to walk up the stairs to my apartment to gather a few of my things to take with me to her house so I sat in the car right outside my front door and waited on them with the doors locked and the engine running, just in case I needed to run over my attacker if I saw him. It was late afternoon, and I figured by now he was probably on the property. Since I had gotten attacked, my senses were extremely high. I paid attention to everything. And after dealing with a failing judicial system, I realized I was the only one who was going to protect myself, and I was the only one who had my best interest at heart.

On our way out of the complex, we drove around back where my truck was parked so I could get a few things out of it. When I opened the door, I noticed a few dried puddles of blood on my seat, and some had made its way to the carpet near the driver door. It reminded me of how much blood had actually made its way through my clothes into my vehicle. I had no idea I bled that much.

While getting my things out, I looked in the direction of my apartment building and saw a moving truck parked nearby. I assumed it was my attacker's guardians in the process of moving out. It felt a little weird knowing that they were only a few feet away from me, but I also felt better knowing that hopefully they'd be gone when I got back. The scary part was that I didn't know where they were going. Having moved from such a large city in Texas, Baton Rouge seemed to be so much smaller this time around. It seemed as if the city was so compact that no matter where they'd move, it would still be much too close to me.

CHAPTER 7

Silent Nights

∽ჟ

*Casting down imaginations, and every high thing
that exalteth itself against the knowledge of God,
and bringing into captivity every thought to the
obedience of Christ. (II Corinthians 10:5)*

IT WAS JUST AFTER DARK when we finally made it to my parent's house. Their home sat on top of a hill in a country neighborhood about five miles outside of town. As always, the nights were rather quiet. I'd hear cars passing on the road until sometime after midnight and then total silence would consume the area for hours.

My first nights at home were pretty rough. I didn't get much sleep. Traditionally, I'd sleep in complete darkness, but now, I'd leave the light on in the bathroom that stood across the hall from my bedroom. I'd anoint my hands and my head with Holy oil and beg God to allow me to at least get a few hours of uninterrupted sleep. He'd grant my request for the first 3 or 4 hours of the night but then I'd wake up. Yes, I was sleeping but I wasn't really resting. I'd wake up tired as if I hadn't gotten any sleep at all.

The silence was sometimes tormenting when I'd wake up in the middle of the night. It was like a force causing me to think, something I didn't want to do. Sometimes, I'd think about what it was going to be like when I'd go back to Baton Rouge. So many questions clouded my mind. Would I be able to conquer staying alone again? Would I be able to walk out my front door in the mornings and go to work? Would I be able to go about my day like I had before? Would I be free to be who I used to be? It was frustrating to hear those questions that forced their way into my mind because I didn't have the answers. I had no idea what I was going to do. There was no easy plan to fix this. I didn't have step-by-step guidance or a play book of what I should do and how I should do it. There was just so much confusion in my head. I hated not knowing how to make it all go away.

In those moments, the only thing I clutched to was the fear that surrounded me in the darkness. It seemed as if fear was the only thing up at that time of night. It seemed to be the only thing that answered my call when I cried, and it was quick to come. Sometimes, the thoughts would get so intense that tears would roll down my face uncontrollably until the sheet underneath me was soaked.

Ravaging thoughts clouded my mind and put even more fear in my heart. What if he comes back? What if this happens again? Sometimes, my thoughts were so overwhelming that when I tried to pray, I felt like I was losing a spiritual battle because I didn't feel like my prayers were getting to God because nothing was changing. I was still in shock, afraid, full of fear, depressed, waking up in the night, overcome with emotions at all times. I felt so defeated. It wasn't like I didn't know the Bible or hadn't studied God's word. I knew the scripture that says to take every thought into captivity that exalted itself against God, but those thoughts were coming at me so fast that it became overwhelming. One right after the other, they came. It was like an evil team was assigned to overtake me, destroy me, and kill me silently.

I never thought something of this magnitude would ever happen to me. I always assumed that if it did, I would be so in oneness with God. I thought I would be such a strong soldier that every time I got hit, I'd be able to swing back and knock my storm down, winning every single time, but it didn't work that way. It seemed like God was so silent. He wasn't saying one word even when I'd beg Him to tell me why He was allowing me to go through this. Even when I begged Him to take the pain away and give me peace, rest, or just a good night sleep. The only confirmation I got was dead silence. I felt like I was in this battle alone and He had actually walked away and left me.

I had always been a dreamer and for years, I dreamt so much at night that I kept a journal next to my bed and every morning, I'd write down my dreams. I used detailed descriptions of everything I saw, touched, or smelled. Many times, God would speak to me through dreams. Sometimes, He even warned me of things to come but for some reason during this time, I wasn't dreaming at all. He wasn't even speaking to me through dreams and I felt so lost and disconnected. Everything I was used to doing to connect with Him didn't seem to work. I just hoped that all the prayers I had ever prayed throughout my life would go up before Him and He would remember them. He would comfort me and give me peace. I often whispered many times, "God please just remember me. Please, don't forget about me."

CHAPTER 8

Therapeutic Moments

*Come unto me, all ye that labour and are
heavy laden, and I will give you rest. Take
my yoke upon you, and learn of me; for I am
meek and lowly in heart: and ye shall find
rest unto your souls. For my yoke is easy, and
my burden is light. (Matthew 11:28-30)*

WHEN MY PARENTS BUILT THEIR home many years ago, it
was a small, two-bedroom house but because of my dad's
carpentry skills, he was always adding on more and more.
When my brothers, sisters, and I came home to visit, we'd
always tease him about rearranging something or adding
something to the house. We might have visited and the
kitchen was on one end with the cabinets all around and a
few years later, he'd move it all to the other end. Someone
would always notice something different whether it was the
change of a window or a door. Now, the house is much
bigger with four bedrooms, two baths, a large den, dining

room, and kitchen. There is also a closed-in patio with windows all around on the other side of the den near the laundry room and the carport.

Usually, my parents made their way out to the patio every morning with their coffee and talked. The following morning when I got up, I didn't hear the mumbling of voices through the door and it bothered me. Having walked through the house once, I came back into the den and called out to my mom because I thought something had happened to them, but I found her standing near the laundry door sweeping the floor. Yes, I panicked because everything that came to mind revolved around fear and violence and the question of "What if." Those were the only things that clouded my mind.

Every morning after that, I'd make my way to the patio, too. It was the hangout spot for us all. My parents would get up much earlier than I did and they'd watch the cars go down the road as people raced to work. They'd listen to the sound of school buses zigzag up and down the roads, picking up kids along the way.

Their house sat on one acre of land. Across the road, a pond sat in a large pasture that ran along the main road for at least a quarter of a mile. There was also a pasture on the south end of the house next to the patio and driveway, which ran down a hill behind the house to another pond. The neighbors who owned those pastures farmed and raised cattle.

Usually during the early mornings, a herd of cows would make their way up the pasture next to our house to start their day. As the sun rose up above the trees, I'd sit and listen to the sound of cows pulling up grass while their little calves playfully ran beside them without a care in the world. I'd watch as those baby calves never strayed too far from their mothers because they knew that their mothers and the bull assigned to shepherd them held a hedge of protection around them. They knew there was always a place of safety for them, and they never seemed to worry about anything—even where their next meal would come.

I wondered what it would be like to feel free without a care in the world, knowing that someone had my back. I longed to feel protected and covered and provided for like those little calves. I felt as if I was in a pasture all alone, exposed to vicious wolves out to get me and take me down. I knew I had a Savior who loved me and longed to protect me, but I felt like He was so far away. I felt like He was unreachable and untouchable and at times, I didn't feel safe and secure.

Sometimes, I'd stay out there for hours and maybe even all day until late evening when dark fell and cars were forced to turn on their headlights. The patio became a rest haven for me. It was therapeutic and I liked it.

Even though the sights and sounds around me gave me a calm, soothing feeling, I still had a lot to worry about. There were still so many things I had to deal with. Three things I kept close beside me were my cell phone, a pen, and a notebook. I had so many business cards, names, and contact numbers, that I couldn't keep them all straight in my head. In between making phone calls and making phone calls again—when people promised to call you back but didn't or you left a message and then left another—my anxiety levels would rise. I knew how many hours of annual leave and sick time I had at work, but I worried about how my budget would look when that ran out. I worried because when I enrolled in my health insurance plan with my job, I didn't enroll in the short term disability and once my sick time ran out, I wouldn't get another paycheck until I returned to work. I worried because I was told by my Human Resource Department that I didn't qualify for FMLA (Family Medical Leave Act) because I hadn't been at my job long enough, and I hadn't accumulated enough hours. So, if my job decided to release me, they could do so at any time. With all those known facts roaming through my head, I still had to deal with the pain of a stab wound that wasn't going to heal overnight. A wound so deep that I was only able to sleep on my back at night and sometimes take medication to keep the pain at a minimum. I was having to eat certain foods to build my blood back up because I had lost so much of it and was still very weak. Every time my anxiety level rose, I felt it in my nerves and my wound would ache. I knew that if I didn't take care of myself, it would take even longer for me to heal, and I'd pay for it in a big way. So I learned that some phone calls that needed to be made and some things on my to-do-list just weren't a priority anymore. I think that is the only way I survived. All I could do was believe that God was going to take care of me and put my trust in Him.

CHAPTER 9

Family Ties

~&~

Behold, we count them happy
which endure. (James 5:11)

FIVE DAYS AFTER I WAS attacked, my three older sisters, my nieces; Jada and Kahrin; and my nephew, Emery, drove down from Texas to visit me. I was so excited to see them because it took my mind off my own problems and allowed me to focus on something else.

They arrived in the early afternoon and filled the house with lots of luggage and laughter. From the looks on my sister's faces, as they each hugged me, I could tell they had been worried about me. I could see it in their eyes. Maybe seeing that I was walking, talking, and breathing gave them some relief and put to rest some questions that they had in their minds about my well-being. Sometimes, family members have such a tight bond that when one person in the family is going through a difficult time, everyone can feel the effects of it. And, for them, it was almost as if each one was stabbed and assaulted and was dealing with it in their own way.

My six-year-old niece, Kahrin, was a ball of energy when she walked inside. I was already prepared for the non-stop talking and all the questions I knew she was going to ask. She wanted to know exactly what happened to me. Her mother had warned me that she really didn't tell her everything or go into any details so, of course, I only told her the story in a mild nutshell because I didn't want to frighten her. I told her that a kid had attacked me, leaving out the fact that he stabbed me with a knife that put me in the ICU. She wanted to know where my injuries were and if they hurt and if was I taking medication. The only visible injury she could see was the cut across my neck and that was the only one I showed her. My stab wounds were still covered up in bandages with stitches in them, and I wasn't going to allow her to see any of that. It might have caused her to ask even more questions that I didn't want to answer. I did, however, confirm with her that I was taking medication but only when I ached. Apparently, she was satisfied with my answers because she didn't drill me with more questions about the incident or my injuries; however, she did decide later on to interview me. Her imagination ran wild and she said she was a news anchor for Fox 4 News coming to me live and wanted to know about my day and how I was doing. She found something lying around the house that she used to represent a microphone and had someone record the interview with her mom's iPad. It was hilarious. My sisters chimed in and she decided to interview Jean as well. Needless to say, Kahrin and Jean have their own unique relationship where they can go toe-to-toe with each other in a humorous way. When she interviewed her, Jean took it up a notch. I guess because Jean was getting all of our attention with her funny stories and comments, Kahrin, within a split second, decided she didn't want to be the news anchor anymore—she wanted to be interviewed as well. As usual, she wanted to be the center of attention. The questions asked and the answers given during their interview were outrageously funny. When the fiasco was all over, we watched the videos over and over, laughing until our sides almost hurt.

My brother, Ron, and his family joined us later that evening. My dad fried fish so we all gathered around in our usual spot on the patio and had dinner together.

Usually, I'm not much of a talker when my entire family is around. I have three older sisters and two older brothers, and with my parents, in-laws, nieces, and nephews, it adds up to almost twenty people within the family. There are some family members who are much more vocal than I am, and they usually stir the conversations. I'm rather quiet but will throw in a few comments here or there. So as usual, on that Saturday afternoon, I sat back and allowed them to take the lead and talk about things that were important to them, their jobs, and their families. It was good to just relax, enjoy them, and learn about things that were going on in their lives. However, we did spend our share of time talking about the incident. I wasn't at all afraid to talk about it. It wasn't like I was near to tears every time I told the story or someone had to tiptoe around me because they would get me emotionally upset. I wanted to talk about it. I wanted an opportunity to get inside of that kid's head and find out why he would do such a thing. Everybody had their own opinion of why they thought he did it and what direction the case would go. At the end of the day, we all still had unanswered questions that we hoped would unfold in time.

Later on, my cousin and her daughter came by. They were the first visitors I had to visit me at home outside of my immediate family. It felt good to know that someone wanted to stop by. I enjoyed their company and we talked late into the night. I was glad they came and hated to see them go. It seemed like that day went by so quick. I guess because my mind was occupied with so much love that was around me.

There is nothing like having family to come together to support a wounded victim. Just to see them there gave me strength. Their presence gave my mind a much-needed vacation from thinking of the things I was dealing with. Just to know that they cared and took time out of their own busy lives to come and check on me was priceless. I couldn't imagine what it would be like to deal with all of this without them.

CHAPTER 10

The Struggles

⤴

Then they cry unto the Lord in their
trouble, and he bringeth them out of
their distresses. (Psalm 107:28)

A week before my attack, for some reason, I went to the store and
bought a purple thermal cup. At the time, I didn't know that my
purple cup would be a tool used to protect me and help save my
life. It stood between my body and the knife of my attacker that
morning as I fought him with everything I had. Now that cup is
displayed on my kitchen counter and every time I pass by, I am
reminded of the life I still have. See, that cup stood in my place
and took some of the knife punctures that could have gone into
my body—four or five deep markings displayed openly. It was
as if God slipped inside that cup and took my place just like He
took my place on Calvary that day, bearing my agony and pain
on the cross, dying in my place for my sins.

Blog Post "Giving Thanks"

ONCE I DRESSED FOR WORK the morning of my incident, I went into the kitchen and fixed myself a cup of hot tea. Sometimes, if I had time, I'd fix a cup and drink it on my way to work. My parents had visited me about two weeks prior during the Labor Day weekend and for some reason, my mom wanted to go to the store and buy herself a thermal cup. She said she'd pack it with ice on her way to her doctor visits during those hot summer days to keep cool. I remember patiently waiting in the cup aisle at the store. For some reason, she just couldn't seem to find the right one. As she sorted through the variety, my dad took an interest in looking for one for himself, too. She picked out this purple cup that she kept close to her but put it back when she and my dad decided to get matching cups. I guess that's the kind of things to look forward to when you've been married to someone for over fifty years. I had no intentions of buying a cup that day but for some reason, I picked up the purple cup she put back and decided to get it. I figured if I didn't get it that day, I'd probably wish I had later on.

I hadn't actually noticed the markings on the cup until a few days after I got home from the hospital. The only reason I took it out of my truck was because it was full of green tea that had been sitting in there since the day I was admitted into the hospital. I didn't realize that there were about five knife punctures on it with spotted blood in several places until I started to examine it. Those punctures were supposed to go inside my body. That was another moment I realized that I was supposed to be dead. I realized my body should have had more than two stab wounds. I wondered what would have happened if I didn't have that cup in my hand that day. I believe with God's help, that cup saved my life. It holds a special place in my heart. I don't display it out in the open much anymore but every time I see it, I am reminded of the life I still have. I am reminded that I get to open up my eyes every day and spend another day with my family and friends.

But, knowing that I am blessed to be alive still didn't stop me from having struggles. It didn't stop me from being human. It didn't stop me from losing faith and feeling like I was drowning in this storm. Some mornings as I dressed for the day, I'd look at myself in the mirror with red, swollen eyes asking God why He was allowing me to go through this. Sometimes, I was so angry at Him because I felt out of everyone, He was supposed to protect and cover me. He wasn't supposed to allow a part of me to die that day. He should have saved me. And, I couldn't figure out for the life of me why He chose this type of battle for me? Who said I was a soldier who could fight a battle as a crime victim. I didn't even know another crime victim. Growing up, I was never exposed to a life of crime. I couldn't even relate to that type of environment. I grew up in church and my parents were evangelists and pastors in ministry. I was from a small town and lived in a neighborhood surrounded by aunts, uncles, cousins, and friends who were just like me. I didn't understand what He was doing. Why would He allow me to deal with so much fear when He knew that I lived alone? How was I supposed to go about living my life as it was before? How was I supposed conquer that giant? Was I supposed to be like David, the shepherd boy, standing in the face of Goliath with a slingshot in my hand? Every time I thought about it, it seemed like all hope was gone.

Other times, I'd blame myself for getting into this situation because I felt like it was my fault. Maybe if I hadn't relocated back to Louisiana, this wouldn't have happened to me. Maybe if I hadn't taken a job with such a huge cut in pay and wasn't living in an apartment but could afford to buy a home with an attached garage, I wouldn't have been walking outside to my vehicle at that time of the morning. Maybe if I had taken a different career path and made more money to support myself or if I was married and had children, I wouldn't be living this type of life. I thought that if I had done things differently early on in my life and made better choices, none of this would have happened to me. I blamed myself all the time and beat myself up constantly. I took my own mental boxing gloves, put them on my own hands, and hit myself in the eyes. I was the cause of my own abuse and body bruises.

In the midst of those struggles, I still had to try to take care of my body. I was very weak and I had lost a lot of blood. I noticed that my eating habits had changed, and I had lost a lot of weight. When I'm depressed, I don't have an appetite for food. At times, it feels like I just want to throw up. It is one of the symptoms I endure although it wasn't until after I was assaulted did I realize that I had created this habit. Everybody deals with depression in their own way. Some people binge-eat while others hardly eat anything at all. It was very hard for me to eat a balanced meal because sometimes I just didn't have a taste or a craving for anything so my body wasn't getting the nutrition that it needed to heal. But, when I finally moved in with my parents, my mom made sure that I ate healthy meals every day, and she kept tabs on me and knew when I'd go into those deep depressions sometimes for days. She'd constantly remind me that I needed to eat something even if it was just a couple of bites. And yes, she would literally go behind me and check. I either did it or else. But I was very blessed because my dad faithfully grew a garden every year and I had the opportunity to eat fresh vegetables on a daily basis.

Now, I don't know what I would have done had my parents not covered me with their prayers and support. I don't know if I would have survived.

The daily phone calls from my family and friends in the days and weeks that followed are what I think kept me going. It didn't resolve the issue or take away the pain, but it just gave me a boost of strength to make it through that one day, and I hoped and prayed that the next day would be a success, too. Joyes was a stay-at-home mom at the time, and she'd call me every day while in the carpool line waiting to pick up her daughter from school. My brother, Tommy, who lived in California, would call me at least once or twice a week to check on me. My co-workers would text me or call to check on me, and that made me feel good. The news had gotten around at work and they were concerned about me and were very supportive. They even sent me a bouquet of flowers and cards saying that they were praying for me and sending me well wishes. And, my dear friend Stephanie, who lived in Texas, would call and talk to me for hours as if we had met at Starbucks across the street. She was one who could really get my mind off my problems, and I love her for that. Not only her, but I appreciated the support that everyone gave to me because I needed it so much. At those moments when I felt like I was at a breaking point, God would always send someone my way to brighten my day.

CHAPTER 11

Facing Fear

~

And the Lord, he it is that doth go before
thee; he will be with thee, he will not fail
thee, neither forsake thee: fear not, neither
be dismayed. (Deuteronomy 31:8)

SATURDAY NIGHT, I FINALLY HAD a dream. I was so surprised that I had one since I wasn't sleeping regularly at night and hadn't dreamt in weeks. In the dream, I rode a bus heading north. While on the bus, I realized that I had so much stuff I needed to carry off that I wore three backpacks. The bus stopped at my destination, but I didn't get off. I continued to gather my things while the driver made his rounds at other stops. I was trying to put smaller things inside large bags so I wouldn't have so much to carry. When the bus driver made his way back to my destination, I still had a lot of stuff but for some reason, none of those things seemed to be too heavy. Everything that I carried on my back seemed to be so light that I hardly felt the weight of it at all.

There were so many more details about that dream, it took up to three pages to write it all down. That Sunday morning, as I sat on my bed in tears and journaled my dream, I made up my mind that the next day, I would pack up my things and go back to my apartment. I didn't tell anyone what I was planning to do because I didn't want anyone to talk me out of it, and I didn't want them to worry. It was either now or never. And, I wanted to do it alone. I wanted to see if I could handle it. I wanted to see if I had the courage to face my fears. No matter how much support I'd have if someone went with me, I knew that I'd still be left alone to deal with this issue weeks or months later because eventually people had to go back to living their own lives. And in the back of my mind, I knew that being dependent on other people can sometimes become an addiction, and I didn't want to be an addict. I wanted to be free. If freedom meant getting in the ring, putting on my boxing gloves, and fighting my way through this, that was what I was determined to do.

The next morning, I got up early and started packing. My eyes were so blurred from tears welling up in them that I could hardly see. I was so angry and frustrated and deep down inside, I was petrified and scared to death. How in the world was I supposed to do this? How was I going to live a free life when I was chained up with so much fear? It just wasn't fair. Why did this have to happen to me?

Now was not the time for me to explore new heights and unknown territories in my life. Now was not the time for me to go to war with fear to understand its tactics and ways. What benefit was I going to gain from it anyway? To be honest, sometimes I'd cringe when I'd listen to others talk about their faith and trusting in an unseen God. I wondered if they had been through what I'd been through, would they make the same statements? I wondered if they had ever been violated almost to the point of death? How would they feel if they had to learn how to fall asleep at night alone with an unseen God who wasn't going to be there in the flesh? I'm sure they had husbands, wives or children who would be there with them every night, and they had garages attached to their homes that they could use to get inside their vehicles. But I had none of that. I was going to have to walk outside every morning alone like I did that Monday morning to get inside my vehicle, and check the doors every single night to make sure they were locked. And God knew all of this. He knew every intimate detail about me and He still allowed this to happen. What lesson was I supposed to learn? Where was He trying to take me in all of this? I felt so trapped because I knew I needed to go back to work to make a living, but I had been violated in a city that gave me financial stability. I just kept telling myself that I had to do this and I had to get back into the swing of things no matter how I felt. Life goes on, I thought, and I was either going to catch on and live or bury myself in a grave.

When I walked into the den and starting filling up the room with suitcases and bags, my parents didn't say anything. I didn't even want them to help me bring my things into the room even though the wound in my liver was still very tender. If God was punishing me and this was my battle to fight, I was supposed to fight it alone.

A little later, my mom asked me if I was leaving and I told her yes. I didn't even want to make eye contact with her. She seemed upset. I could see it in her face but she didn't say anything. She just turned around and went into the kitchen and started packing up leftovers from the refrigerator for me to take. When she finished packing up the food, she came outside and helped me pack my things inside my truck that I picked up a few weeks ago from my apartment when I went to Baton Rouge for a doctor's appointment.

My dad was sitting on the patio but came inside before I left. He didn't have an opinion about me leaving but asked a question or two to confirm. I nodded. He wanted to have prayer so he and my mom and I held hands and prayed. I cried so hard standing there, knowing that I was on my way into the unknown. I didn't know how I was going to deal with this. I had no idea how this was going to work out. I had no plan. I had nothing.

After making sure I had packed everything and said my goodbyes, I climbed into my vehicle with uncontrollable, silent tears racing down my face, the kind that keeps coming until they roll down your chin onto your neck.

As I backed out, I saw my mom standing outside the door under the carport with her hand over her heart. I knew she was scared for me. I saw it in her eyes. I knew that if she could, she would have jumped in that truck and come with me. I knew she wanted to protect me because that is what mother's do. But somehow I had to figure this one out on my own.

The hour-and-a-half drive gave me time to settle my nerves. The departure from my parent's house was very discomforting for me. It wasn't an easy task to complete. I'm sure my parents probably thought I was making an emotionally crazy decision, but they have always allowed their children to test the waters. I hoped they understood what I was doing and the reasoning behind it, but I didn't do such a good job of explaining myself to them that day. I was more frustrated than anything, some things I said may not have come across in the right manner. I was worried about them. I knew that they both had hypertension and I didn't want their blood pressure to rise in any way. So I said a prayer hoping that they would at least get a couple of hours of sleep that night even if I didn't.

The manager at the complex had contacted me several weeks ago and told me that my attacker and his guardians had moved out, and my parking space was in the front parking area just outside my door. I was thankful for that but even though he was gone, I was still uncomfortable not knowing where he was. I had made a decision not to move to another apartment just yet because I didn't know where they were, and I was afraid I'd run into them. I was comfortable at this apartment, knowing that all the employees and the courtesy officers knew what had happened to me and would keep an eye on me.

I made it to the complex around one o'clock in the afternoon. Some of the maintenance workers at the property used a few of the storage garages in front of my apartment building to work on appliances that needed servicing. One in particular that I was very familiar with was outside when I arrived. I wouldn't say that I trusted him but I was secretly more comfortable with him than any of the others. I got a sense of peace when I'd see him around even though we never held a conversation with each other but always said a friendly "hello". So, I thanked God for answering my prayer. On my way, I asked Him not to allow me to be alone so that I could unload my stuff when I arrived, and He did just that. During the middle of the day, it is extremely quiet at the complex and there isn't a lot of foot traffic going on, and I didn't want anyone sneaking up on me while I was trying to unload my stuff. I wanted people around just in case I needed to scream for help. Maybe this time, someone would rescue me or drive someone away who was trying to hurt me. And with the maintenance worker being there and knowing my situation, I figured I could depend on him to help.

My anxiety levels went up a couple of notches when I opened my truck door to get out. I was so nervous walking up the stairs to open my front door that I was literally shaking. I still remember it clearly in my head. I tried to be quiet, listening and positioning myself so no one would walk up behind me.

I was able to get a few loads out of my truck while the maintenance guy worked outside but then he left, so the rest of the stuff remained in there for several hours. I had so much stuff, and it seemed like I brought back twice as much.

It started to rain later on that day. It was around four o'clock before I finished unloading. I waited until people started to get off work and come home because I felt comfortable seeing them out walking or getting out of their cars or going to check their mailboxes. The more people I saw outside, the better I felt when I was out there with them.

As soon as I made it to the apartment, I called my mom. She seemed fine on the other end of the phone. I guess we both just needed some time to settle our nerves. I didn't call any of my other family members because I didn't want them worried about me.

Things were fine after I got everything inside and unpacked, keeping myself busy until it started to get dark. I didn't like it when the sky started to dim. Even though my apartment was tiny and I kept the majority of my lights off, I still didn't like it. Something about nightfall made me nervous. I remember sitting on my floor looking through my bedroom window to see what kind of activity was going on outside. I didn't want anyone to see me standing up in the window so I sat on the floor. I had never worried about noises going on outside, people talking, cars passing by, or doors slamming. As long as it wasn't something near my front door, it didn't bother me. But, now, everything mattered. I had to check everything. I even contemplated when would be the best time to take a shower. Were the mornings good after everyone else was at work and the nights too bad knowing that my neighbors around me could hear the faucet running? I felt like someone could be watching me at all times, knowing my every move—when I come and when I go. I considered myself a watchman on the wall, determined to stay hidden and safe.

I ate something, watched a little TV, and finally decided to lie down and try to get some rest. I felt comfortable leaving my TV on all night for noise, but I wasn't comfortable sleeping on my sofa so I'd turn it up loud enough to hear it in my bedroom. With the lights off, I could see the colorful reflections from the TV come through my door and hit my walls. When I'd wake up in the middle of the night, it seemed to be so loud that I assumed my neighbors could hear it. But, for me, I had to survive. I had to find a way to make this work.

Each night before I lay down, I'd turn the channel to Daystar, a Christian television station, because I needed something positive flowing. I couldn't risk waking up in the middle of the night to the sound of some movie scaring me half to death. Usually, when I'd wake up, I'd hear the sound of praise and worship songs from a nightly program that lasted for several hours called "Reflections." One song sometimes woke me up out of my sleep called "I Give You

My Heart" by Joni Lamb and the Daystar Singers. For the first several nights, I remember hearing the song but when I'd wake up the next day, I couldn't remember the lyrics. Sometimes, even when I wasn't fully awake, I'd hear that song playing and it sounded like angels singing. I remember some nights waking up waiting for the song to play, and it didn't happen. So, for a moment, it was a mystery to me. But, once I got familiar with the song, I'd hear it, get up, and go into my living room and sit on the floor and weep. I'd sit there and think about all those moments when I didn't have enough faith to completely trust God. Those moments when I became angry at Him. Those moments when I worried about how I was going to walk out my front door in the mornings without fear or when I allowed depression to consume me. I felt bad for not totally trusting Him because I was supposed to be a Christian. I was supposed to be the one who trusted God no matter what. I was supposed to remember every battle-fighting scripture and stand on each of them. But I had been beaten down and stripped of almost everything, and I was worn and weak. I knew I needed to have faith in Him even more and surrender every bit of fear and anger and all those other emotions I had bottled up inside of me, but sometimes, it seemed so hard to do. There were those moments when I saw my opponent much stronger than me. Sometimes that was my reality especially when I was alone. It wasn't as simple as some might think. It was difficult and I was just trying to survive.

CHAPTER 12

Breakthrough

—⸜⸝—

He maketh the storm a calm, so that the
waves thereof are still. (Psalm 107:29)

IN THE DAYS THAT FOLLOWED, I didn't feel very well.
I think I tried to carry too many things up the stairs at
once and overdid it because my wound ached a lot. It felt
strained and open inside. My abdominal area was very sore
and I could hardly lift anything. If I did, I could feel the
effects of it. So for the next several days, I lay around trying to give my body a break. But, even on those days that
I rested, I was thoroughly entertained by family members
through the phone calls I received. One day, I talked for a
total of eight hours on the phone. Yes, eight hours. Once
my brothers and sisters found out that I had returned to
the apartment, one after the other, they would call telling
me about their day and what was going on in their lives.

But, I didn't mind it at all. I was grateful for their company because it kept my mind occupied.

After I closed my front door when I first got back, I didn't open it again until seven days later. I wasn't progressing so well. I was locked up inside and I couldn't get out. It became a mental war, a battle going on inside my head. Every day, I'd get up and make plans to go out and run errands, but I could never seem to put my hand on the doorknob, turn it, and walk out. In my mind, something was always wrong. I'd look out the window and use the excuse that no one was outside or it was too late in the afternoon to go anywhere. Thank God I had enough food and water to survive those seven days; otherwise, I don't know what I would have done. It was as if a spirit of fear had a strong hold on me and wasn't about to let go. Almost like it had boarded up my front door on the outside with hammer and nails, and captured me.

One night when I got ready for bed, I checked my front door to make sure it was locked. I had formed a habit of checking that door over and over again just to make sure that it was actually shut tight and I was safely secured inside. It was around midnight when I went to the door one last time just to confirm again when suddenly someone bumped up against it. It sounded like someone's jacket hit the door, like the sound of a zipper, as if they were throwing it over their shoulder. I was standing at the door, eye to eye with the deadbolt lock, when it happened, and my knees started to tremble. My heart pounded so loud that the sound came out through my ears and I imagined everyone in the complex could hear it. It was one of the most terrifying feelings I have ever experienced. I was so afraid that I sprinted into my bedroom with my phone in one hand and my pepper spray in the other. Other than God's angels watching over me, that was the only physical protection I had. When I got into the bedroom, I just stood there for a moment, not knowing what to do, trying to come up with a plan just in case someone barged in on me. Because there was only one main entrance into the apartment, the only option I quickly thought of was to open up the patio door in my living room and tumble over the balcony of my second story apartment. But for the moment, I just stood there in silence with my hand over my heart waiting for the person on the other side of that door to make their next move. Thank God nothing happened. I was only at the mercy of God's grace that night because I wasn't even sure if I could defend myself if I needed to. I didn't even know if I had the strength to go through another assault again. Still shaken up, I didn't even change into my pajamas before getting into bed. I slept afraid and fully clothed. I don't know how I managed to get any sleep that night but somehow I did. It was only by the grace of God.

On Sunday, day seven, I got up and decided to wash my hair. When I really didn't feel like doing my hair, I'd complete the process in two steps. First, I'd wash and dry it then, later on, I'd flat iron it. That day, I got a phone call from Marcella before I was able to start ironing it. She said she was out and wanted to know what I was up to. I told her that I was doing my hair and I had planned to go out and run some errands (not really). I gave her the impression that my entire day had been planned out but I knew within myself that I probably wasn't even going to get out the door. But, before I knew it, she was texting me saying that she was driving into the apartment complex. Although I really wasn't prepared, her arrival gave me the push to finish what I was doing, get dressed, and get out. Looking back, I like how God handled that situation. Sometimes, we don't need a plan. Sometimes we need to be thrusted into doing something to break a chain that has us tied up.

Walking out that front door for the first time with Marcella reminded me of a bird soaring in mid-air after fleeing from a birdcage. Yes, I was afraid, but I felt so much freedom to just breathe and get out. To be among the living and not stuck between walls was priceless. Marcella had no idea what she did when she pulled me out of the apartment that day. She had no idea that the trip we took to the store gave me a push, a determination that I could possibly do this alone. It was my breakthrough moment. When I walked across the threshold of the door, I was terrified. Marcella had no clue what kind of inward battle I was fighting. She was laughing and talking as she went out the door but I wasn't. For sure, I thought someone was going to come out of nowhere and grab her. I wanted to warn her and tell her to be careful but she carried no sense of fear at all. There were no boundaries holding her back. She wasn't boxed in a cage with fear. She was free. Seeing her that way made something break inside of me. I felt a release. I knew that if she could walk out the door, so could I.

While riding in the truck with her, I remember taking deep breaths, trying to suck it all in—trying to get as much air into my nostrils to take back with me behind those four walls. Maybe if I craved it enough, I'd want it so bad that I'd force myself to open up that front door and walk out alone next time.

"ME"

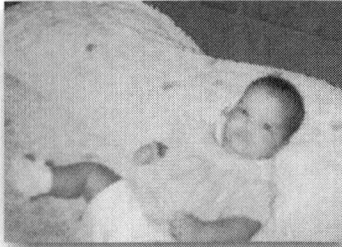

I was about 6 months old and yes I was
born with very little hair.

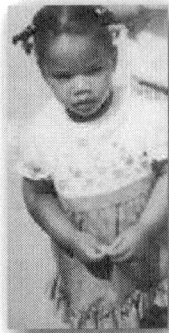

My mom took my brother and I to school that day to
see my sister Joyes. She was a sunflower in a play.

My mom made my suit and hair bows. I
thought I was pretty cute that day.

Pine High School Homecoming Queen. Go Raiders!

Southeastern Louisiana University Graduate, B.S. Accounting,

"MY FAMILY"

Mom and Dad.

Sisters Joyes, Janice and Jean.

Brother Tommy.

Brother Ron, niece Mia and sister-in-law Elisa.

Nephews Ron Jr, and Jamie, and niece Mia.

Nephews Emery and Evan, and niece Jada.

My talkative niece Kahrin.

Hanging out with my sisters during lunch after
one of my speaking engagements.
I love spending time with them.

"My Journey"

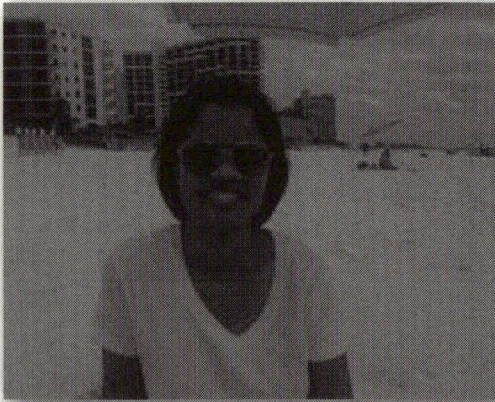

About two weeks after my incident. My
sister Jean took me to the beach.

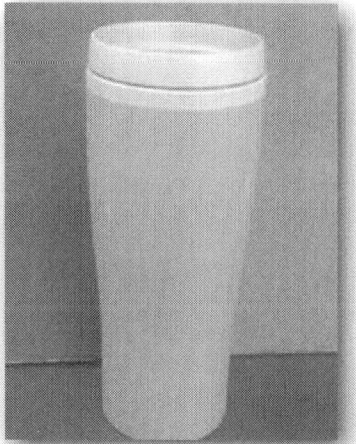

You probably can't see the knife punctures but this is the purple cup I was carrying the morning of my attack.

Lunch with my family the day of sentencing.

Moving into the Light Support Group certificate of completion along with a poem given to me about purpose and of course the best book in the world…my bible.

Moving into the Light Support Group graduation day and Balloon Ceremony.

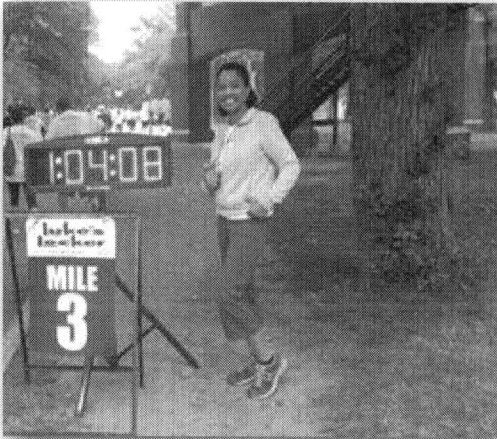

Victory Over Violence 5K Walk in Fort Worth,
TX sponsored by The Women's Center to support
domestic violence victims and their families.

First speaking engagement at The Women's Center during the
National Crime Victims Rights' Week in Fort Worth, TX.

Here and now. Still standing strong.

CHAPTER 13

Hostage

~⤸~

They mount up to the heaven, they go down
again to the depths: their soul is melted
because of trouble. (Psalm 107:26)

MONDAY, I CALLED MY DOCTOR because I needed to go to his office and drop off some forms for him to complete. I explained to the nurse what I needed and that I was going to stop by the next day, drop them off, and pick them up when they were ready. I figured that would give me an excuse to get out of the house at least two days that week. I had a plan and I hoped it would work.

The next day, I got up and got dressed to leave. I remember sitting down in my living room fully dressed with my purse and keys in hand watching TV wondering if I was ever going to make a move to get up and open the front door. I think I sat there for at least an hour or two trying to decide. I kept looking out the window to see if anybody was outside. Sure enough, the one maintenance guy that I was comfortable with was working. Had I not seen him, I probably would have used the excuse that no one was outside and stayed home. Since that plan failed, I started mentally preparing and telling myself that I could do this. I slowly, but finally, cracked open the door and glanced outside. With the pounding of my heart, I could feel fear gripping me and saying, "Don't do it," but I ignored it. When I saw that no one was around, I walked out, hurriedly locked the door, and ran down the stairs. My entire body was shaking by the time I reached my truck. All I remember is jumping inside and locking the doors. My heart was beating so loud, it felt like it was in my throat. At that moment, it didn't matter how I felt. I just kept telling myself that I did it. I actually did it! It didn't matter if I was scared or that fear was riding on my shoulders; this was my first time walking out that door alone and I did it. I made a step and it was a start. I had no idea how I was going to get back inside but at least I took a leap of faith and acted on it. I was so proud of myself.

Because I didn't receive a return phone call from the nurse Wednesday morning, I decided to get out that day. I needed to go to the mall. I figured it was a safe place to be with lots of people around. In the back of my mind, I felt like if someone bothered me and I screamed surely someone would hear me inside of the four walls of the mall. Having gone out the day before, I felt a little more confident that morning. I felt like if I'd get out again and again, I'd make more progress. I'd gain more strength and defeat this spirit of fear that was tugging at me.

Usually, when I went to the mall, I'd park only at the store I needed to go to and then leave. But, that day, I decided to look around at a few stores scattered throughout the building. I figured I'd make the most of my day window shopping and getting some much needed fresh air.

When I made my last round, I couldn't remember the directions to the store where my vehicle was parked but I noticed a map display near one of the mall entrances. As I scanned the map, a young lady came up to me. I didn't even see or hear her walk up, so she startled me when I noticed her.

"Do you know her?" she asked me.

"Know who?" I said.

"That girl that is walking out the door."

I looked toward the door and I didn't see anyone.

"She asked me if you and I were roommates. And I told her no," she said. "I told her that I didn't know you."

"No, I don't know her," I said, clutching the pepper spray bottle on my keyring. I didn't know this young lady and I had no idea what her intentions were. She had no idea how much danger she was in because if she attempted to attack me someone was going down and it wasn't going to be me. I had made that clear in my head from the start. Within seconds she was going to transform from an individual with perfectly healthy eyesight to someone who could possibly become severely blind because my plan was to spray that entire bottle of solution into her eyes until no more would come out. At this stage in my life when something unusual and strange happened, my first instinct was to survive and worry about everything else later. That was one of the reason I hadn't purchased a handgun at that time. I was afraid I would possibly harm an innocent person assuming they were out to attack me and I'd have to pay the consequences of it later.

"I told her that I didn't know you. I just thought that was kind of weird for her to ask me that." She wore an odd smirk on her face that didn't sit well with me.

I gave her a slight smile, watching her very closely, and shook my head and said, "No, I don't know her." I never saw anyone at the door at all.

"Oh well," she said, smiling, and then she walked away.

I didn't know what to think. It didn't really faze me at that moment. The situation really dawned on me later on after I got home. Maybe God allowed it to happen that way. For some reason, when I thought about it sitting on my couch, fear consumed me. I didn't know what to do so I called my mom. I told her what happened and I started sobbing. Why were people watching me? Why were they having conversations about me? Why, if I didn't know who they were? I felt overwhelmed. I thought I was making progress by walking out the door and getting out of the house. But every time I took one step forward, it seemed like I was dragged two steps back fighting this battle with fear. I just wasn't gaining ground no matter how hard I tried. She tried to calm and console me by saying that maybe they thought I was someone else. It didn't matter. I just couldn't do this anymore. From the incident of someone hitting my front door late at night to what happened at the mall, it was just too much for me. The breakthrough that I had earlier in the week seemed to have been washed away. It was as if fear wasn't going to let me have a moment of victory.

He was putting pressure on me and sending signals telling me to back off. He wasn't going to give up that easy and he wasn't going down without a fight. He was assigned and determined to take me out. At that moment, I realized that this battle was way too much for me. It was much bigger than I imagined. I was being held hostage by fear.

When my mom couldn't get through to me, she put my dad on the phone. I told him what happened at the mall and he prayed. Immediately, the fear went away. Immediately! In that instance, it was gone and I was at peace. There was a calmness that changed the atmosphere and filled the room. I learned that this relationship with fear was tormenting, and I was going to have to use more than one technique to conquer it. Although I was going to have to continue to open up that front door and go out, I was also going to have to have others stand in my corner with me and hear them pray over me. Because every time I was in a similar situation and prayed, it felt like nothing happened. I was giving it all I had and nothing was changing. But, when my dad prayed, it seemed like everything changed within seconds. And, I needed to know that prayer still worked.

Still determined to defeat fear, the next day, I went out again. The nurse called me and told me that the documents were ready and I could come pick them up. Yes, I was afraid. Very, very afraid. I stood at that door again, telling myself that I could do it. I wasn't going to let fear beat me, yoke me, and lock me up inside. I was determined to win this war. I didn't know what all I was going to go through or how it was going to end but at that moment, I knew I had to keep fighting.

CHAPTER 14

Making Progress

∼⤙

*I press toward the mark for the prize of the high
calling of God in Christ Jesus. (Philippians 3:14)*

MY PARENTS MOVED IN WITH me for a couple of weeks.
Jean also came back and spent another week with me. As
long as they were around, things were fine. I would come
and go without a problem. I'd sleep all night and be re-
freshed in the mornings. The days and weeks between
those times were rough for me because when no one was
there, I had to learn all over again how to handle being
alone. I had to deal with fear again. When family members
left, fear drug its ugly luggage back inside and moved in.
It was a struggle, but even those times got a little better. I
wasn't fully comfortable, but each round got a little lighter.

I remember my dad walking me out the first morning
I went back to work. It was my first time getting out of
the house that early in the morning. I had spoken with my

supervisor and he was willing to work with me and allow me to come in an hour later when daylight was present. Even with my dad watching over me, I was still nervous. Once I got in the truck and locked my door, I wanted him to go back inside. I wanted to make sure he was safe, but he wouldn't. He'd stand around and wait for me to drive off and get completely out of sight before he made a move.

On my first day back at work, I was excited to see everyone. I felt like I was becoming a normal person again. My co-workers had gotten together and sent me flowers, cards, monetary support, and well wishes while I was out, and I thanked them for it all. I was grateful for their thoughtfulness and help. It meant so much to me.

Going back to work kept my mind occupied and I liked that. I wanted to be normal so bad that I tried to push my emotions and pain out of the way, but it just lingered more. I wanted this storm to be over so bad. I just wanted my life back. I wanted things to be the way they used to be. I was sick and tired of it all. I figured by now I'd be over it, but I wasn't. I thought that when I went back to work and got into the swing of things, life's puzzle pieces would fall back into place—at least some of them—but it didn't work that way. I didn't know that the days ahead were going to be just as hard if not harder.

A few weeks later, I got a called from the District Attorney's Office. The prosecutor assigned to my case scheduled a meeting with me. The night before, Janice, who worked for the Tarrant County District Attorney's

Office in Fort Worth, Texas, went over some possible questions I could ask. Having worked with the district attorney for years, she walked me through some procedures and explained to me some of the possibilities that may occur with the case. She made things a lot easier for me. I was glad to know that I wasn't going to walk into something I knew absolutely nothing about. She reminded me to not set my expectations too high because sometimes, it just doesn't work in the victim's favor. I had heard that same statement from the Victim Assistant Coordinator so I wasn't so surprised this time around. I made a mental note of what she said but I knew someone that I could talk to who answered prayers, and I was going to let Him take control of the situation.

The next day, my brother, Ron, met me at work and we drove to the detention center. One of the detectives met us outside and took us into a conference room where we waited for the prosecutor. A few minutes later, she walked into the room with an arm full of folders—juvenile cases she had been reviewing all day long. It was unthinkable, the number of people involved with the judicial system at such a young age. She seemed overloaded with cases because it took her a minute to pull my attacker's file and review it.

She started the meeting off by asking me to tell her what happened. She said that when she read my case, it gave her chills and caused her to be a little more careful of her own surroundings. As she opened up, I became more comfortable with her. She explained that my attacker was released the day after the arrest and that he was placed on house arrest, required to wear an ankle device and was being monitored by his probation officer with surprise visits. I asked her if he was possibly still attending school, and she explained that normally if a juvenile hasn't been convicted of a crime, they are allowed to remain in the school until a court decides their sentence. I asked her that because I knew the school he attended was not far from my house. And if he was still attending school there, I knew he'd have access to where I lived. He could easily hop off the bus at any time and enter the property. I didn't like that at all because I didn't know if his intent was to come back and finish me off or what. I asked her a few of the questions that my sister and I discussed about Louisiana law and how the judicial system worked. She was truthful, realistic, and never made any promises.

Before we left, she showed us the courtroom. I guess she wanted me to be mentally prepared the day of court and I was glad that she did because it was a very small room. I was expecting it to be much larger than that. I realized that my attacker was going to be sitting much closer to me than I imagined. She explained that there were two halls and they would bring him through the back hall so I wouldn't have any contact with him until he entered the courtroom. She gave me all her contact information and we left.

A few days later was Veteran's Day, and the company I worked for was closed in honor of it. I had been doing pretty good going in and out of the apartment on my own. Sometimes, it was still a challenge but for the most part, I was making some progress. After I ate breakfast that morning, I sat around and watched TV for a while. Some maintenance employees at the complex worked on the apartment next door to me. I could hear several of them going in and out. Apparently, one of the maintenance workers got confused as to which apartment they had been working in and all of a sudden, I saw my doorknob turning. I knew the doorknob and deadbolt were both locked, but fear shot up inside of me anyway. I couldn't move. I assumed fear was making his rounds, trying to see if he could settle back inside me once again. He still hadn't given up hope. It seemed as if he was still waiting for his prey, but I was determined to defeat him with everything I had. So I just sat there and kept telling myself that the door was locked. Finally, my nerves started to settle down. It was weird seeing my anxiety levels go from zero to one hundred in just a few seconds. From being perfectly comfortable to having every muscle in your body tense up was devastating.

When I came home the evening before, there was a note posted on my door from a police officer asking me to call him. I didn't return the call, but he came back the next day anyway to serve me with a subpoena for court. I was a little hesitate opening my front door for him even though he was a part of law enforcement. I think he noticed that I was a little nervous but tried to make light of it. It felt weird having a stranger at my front door. Since my incident, I hadn't had any visitors at my apartment other than family and friends, and I hadn't encountered anyone in close proximity to me that I didn't know. I felt a little uncomfortable and I was glad that he handed me the paper quickly and left.

Closing my front door, it felt funny holding the subpoena in my hand with my attacker's name on it. Finally, I was able to identify him by his name and not just as my attacker. The name of John Q. Carter was stamped on the subpoena. He had been known to me as my attacker for so long that I didn't know what to make of it. I didn't know how to react to the fact that he actually had a name. The tears started to roll and I don't really know why. I couldn't figure out if it was because I could finally put a name with a face or because someone with a nice name like John tried to kill me. I couldn't really explain it. But, for some reason, it made me emotional and I cried.

CHAPTER 15

Court

∽

*And this is the confidence that we have in
him, that, if we ask any thing according to
his will, he heareth us. (I John 5:14)*

*When my name is called and I take the stand, I wonder if
my nerves will get the best of me. I wonder if I will be able to
remember every detail.*

*As the countdown continues, reality sets in and it doesn't
feel so good. It doesn't feel good to think about the fact that I'll
have to dig deep down in my soul and remember the details
of that dreadful day. To relive that dark morning is really
something I don't want to face. There are so many layers of
my emotions wrapped around that moment—emotions that
I don't want to disturb—and emotions that I'd like to keep
buried inside.*

*The most terrifying part of it all is walking into that
courtroom and coming face to face with my attacker, coming*

face to face with someone who tried to take my life—with
someone who tried to muzzle my mouth shut, who ignored
my screams and fought with me until I fell to the ground to
complete his mission. When I see him, I wonder if my heart
will beat so loud that everyone in the room will hear it. When
I look him in the face, I wonder if I will get the answers that
I need to try to put the broken pieces of my life back together
again. Will he tell me why he did this to me? Will he tell me
why he took a piece of my soul away from me? Will he tell me
anything at all?

Blog Post: "Setback"

THE DAY OF MY FIRST court appearance, my tiny apartment
was packed with family. It was a cool but sunny November
day. Because Kahrin came down from Texas with my sisters, my mother decided to stay with her while we went to
court. She didn't think it was an appropriate place for her
to be while others discussed the description of a violent
crime.

Before we left, we held hands and prayed. My dad
asked God for favor in the case and to help John admit his
wrongdoings. When he finished making his request, we all
agreed with a strong amen and left knowing that God was
going to intervene.

The prosecutor didn't want me at the detention center until my case was heard to avoid being in contact with

John outside the courtroom, so my family and I hung out nearby. She promised to call me when the judge was ready to hear the case and that ended up being about two hours after my scheduled appointment.

When we got to the detention center, my doctor was there. Also, the lieutenant who handled my case was there along with the witness who heard me screaming that morning. Everybody showed up with no complaints and the prosecutor was pleased that my doctor waited patiently for several hours because usually, the doctors complained and threatened to contact their attorneys for wasting their valuable time. They didn't like being subpoenaed for court. But, I thanked God for my doctor's patience and his concern for me.

Before we went in front of the judge, the prosecutor and her boss called me into the conference room to discuss the case. She said that the defense attorney presented a plea to her for John of a much lesser charge than the original battery charge set at the initial hearing, and she refused it. She said it wasn't even worth discussing with me or having a conversation about it. She said he then came back with another plea of attempted manslaughter and she wanted to know how I felt about accepting those charges. She explained that the judge sitting on the bench was very lenient with juvenile sentencing and she had too much compassion for them. If I rejected the plea, went to trial, and allowed her to make the decision, they couldn't guarantee anything. I didn't know what to do and I wanted to make the best decision possible, so I asked for my family to come into the conference room to get their thoughts. The prosecutor and her boss left the room for a little while. When they returned, we asked several questions and I felt comfortable accepting the plea. Even though I accepted it, I didn't know how his sentencing would fair in regard to the length of time he would serve and decided to leave all that in God's hands.

When the judge returned from recess, my family and I followed the prosecutor down the hallway through some doors to the courtroom. Along the hall sat dozens of kids waiting to go before the judge—kids who had somehow formed a relationship with the law and the judicial system. It was a sad sight. None of them looked worried at all. Some of them acted as if they were angry with the world while others talked to their fellow peers as if they were at the movies waiting for their favorite motion picture to start. I saw mothers and grandmothers there trying to help take care of the affairs of a troubled child in the absence of fathers. As I walked past, the situations along the hall painted devastating pictures of the future. I wondered if we could count on these kids to become law-abiding citizens or if we would spend our tax dollars supporting them behind bars. Would they possibly turn their lives around and make something of themselves? I really didn't know the answer put I hoped and prayed they would. Although they started making wrong choices at such a young age, I hoped that they would be given a second chance at life and take every opportunity available to them. I prayed that they wouldn't be a juvenile standing in front of the judge waiting to be sentenced, but one day they would be the judge sitting on a bench holding the gavel in their own hands.

The pews on the left side of the courtroom where my family and I sat, along with my doctor, the lieutenant, and the witness, had little room left for anyone else to squeeze in. The pews on the right side of the courtroom were filled with a few court employees and a bailiff, but no additional family members of John's were present other than his guardians who sat up front at the table next to him, the probation officer and the defense attorney.

It started to make since why everyone sitting out in the hallway stared at my family and I as we walked toward the courtroom. I guess they had never seen so many family members there playing a supportive role before. Even mothers and grandmothers stopped in the middle of their conversations and looked up at us puzzled. There was so many of us that one young girl told another that we were a jury there for a case not understanding that a supportive caring family makes the difference of where life can lead you. Maybe she had never seen anything like that before. Maybe it was uncommon in her world.

I wasn't as nervous as I thought I'd be when John walked in the courtroom. He looked pretty much the same, skinny with a narrow face and a small-framed body that was only an inch or so taller than mine. He wore slacks and a white, button-down dress shirt. He looked as if he was a member of an elite debate team going before an audience to discuss a matter such as the importance of education and staying in school, but everyone knew that wasn't the case. The appearance on the outside was far different from the darkness he carried on the inside.

The guardians were interviewed by the court first. They were asked to state their names and age. They were a young couple in their mid-twenties. Then they were asked to state their complete address. When they opened their mouths, I was shocked to find out that John lived less than a mile from me, and I shopped less than one hundred yards from the apartment he shared with them. Years ago, before I moved to Texas, I lived in that same complex for about three years. The question that I had asked myself for some time and the answer I needed to hear about whether I wanted to stay in my apartment or move came to fruition while I sat in the courtroom digesting the address. There was no way I was going to remain at my current residence. There should be some law regarding the distance a victim of an assault lives from the one who attacked them. Yes, I was told by the investigator who sat with the prosecutor during our meeting that John was informed not to come around me after he was originally charged, but for me, that wasn't enough. It only took him two seconds to ruin my life and if he wanted to, he could come back. Wearing an ankle monitor meant absolutely nothing. It didn't protect any-one from getting killed. It was only there to track the location of his steps.

When the judge was informed that the defense had of-fered a plea and I accepted it, John was forced to admit what he did. He politely told, verbatim, the same exact story I had told over and over again. He said that he had stalked me for several weeks prior to the attack, knowing exactly what time I left in the mornings. He said that he waited for his younger brother to leave their apartment and walk out to the bus stop, and he got a kitchen knife and put it inside his pocket. Once he attacked me, he threw the knife in the bushes near the storage garages and ran. He said I scared him when I jumped up and ran after him screaming. He noticed a woman out with her dog that morning when he ran around the complex and out the gate, and he was so scared that he hid behind some tall hedges outside the gate until his bus came.

He admitted that he stabbed me but strongly denied the fact that he was the cause of all of my bodily injuries. "Yes, I stabbed Ms. Robinson" he said, "but I didn't do all of that" insinuating that he didn't place the stab wound near my armpit or the cut across my neck. The words flow-ing from his mouth showed his level of maturity. How can he justify one and deny the others when it all happened at the same time?

I could see compassion engulfing the middle-aged judge while she sat in her seat wearing her black robe. She asked him in a still voice, almost in a whisper, why he did that to someone, and he told her because he wanted to know what it felt like. When those words came out of his mouth, the courtroom gasped.

Who in their right mind would want to kill someone? And, what fourteen-year-old made plans to do such a thing? In that moment, I concluded without any doctor's diagnosis that he had serial killer potential. He could live and dwell in society without anyone knowing that he had such thoughts going through his mind because the morning he attacked me, I didn't get a vibe at all that he was about to do something horrific.

She asked him several other questions and he answered her with a "yes ma'am" or "no ma'am," reply portraying to be the proper child that he was not. She advised the defense to schedule a psychiatric evaluation before sentencing.

Because he pleaded guilty to the charges, none of my witnesses or I had to testify. Before our court session started, the prosecutor informed my doctor that I took a plea and tried to convince him to leave, but he refused. I think everyone was interested in hearing this case because it was such a mystery. John made no attempt to rob me and steal my wallet or my purse, even after I fell to the ground. He had a mission to do only one thing. Kill me.

Sometimes I wondered if he would have taken my life and no one ever found out that he killed me, would he have struck again? I wondered if he would have been so daring to do such a thing.

The prosecutor tried to convince the judge to set a bond for John since he pled guilty to manslaughter charges in hopes that he would remain in jail until his sentencing, but she refused. She allowed him to remain on house arrest with the ankle bracelet. My trust in the judicial system to protect citizens was very minimal, then. He still had the opportunity to harm someone else. Instead of myself, I worried more for others who had no idea what this individual was capable of.

They instructed John and his guardians to leave the courtroom before I did. I watched him as he got up and started toward the door. Then, he scanned the row that my sisters and I sat on, being that we all resemble one another in some way until he found me and looked me dead in the face. It didn't frighten me and I didn't get chills. Actually, I felt nothing at all as he looked at me. I didn't have compassion for him, nor did I want him to burn in hell. He had his own set of issues that were far deeper than mine because, to do what he did to me, he had to have a heart of a stone. There was more brewing underneath his skin than the eye could see and obviously he had to have some confusion going on inside that head of his that no one could explain. In my heart, I decided to let God be the judge of him and not me. I didn't want to carry that weight upon my shoulders. I had enough to worry about myself.

A few minutes later, we all got up and went outside into the hall. I thanked my doctor for coming as he gave me a hug and told me to take care of myself. I shook hands with the lieutenant and thanked the witness for taking the time to come.

By the time we arrived back at my apartment, it was early evening and dark. The day before after my sisters came into town, we went to the grocery store and bought food. Joyes cooked a huge pot of delicious red beans and we had plenty left over for the next day. After we got back from court, Jean and I decided to go out and buy our favorite Popeyes chicken to go along with the rest of our meal. With some of the money I received as a financial gift from co-workers, I was able to feed my family. It was the least I could do for them taking off work and driving down to be with me. I was so thankful that they all came. It was a funny sight to see us all cramped up inside my 600 sq. ft. apartment including my parents, my sisters, niece, brother and sister-in-law and myself eating chicken and left over red beans in paper plates. Grant it, I never entertained people at my place at all but I made the best with what I had. Only one couch and a matching chair stood on my living room floor so we found ourselves sitting anywhere we could find a spot. But all in all, we were happy and all smiles. The food was good and everyone was enjoying themselves talking about the case. It is in those moments when I keep sentimental memories like that close at heart.

That night I laid down thinking about the day and what happened. I took a deep breath and felt like I was near the end of this horrific storm that had consumed my life for far too long. It had only been less than three months, but it felt like an eternity. But I learned that this storm wasn't about to be over at all, though; there was so much more to come.

CHAPTER 16

Transitioning

~⤴~

Where no counsel is, the people fall:
but in the multitude of counsellors
there is safety (Proverbs 11:14)

FEAR FOUND ITS WAY BACK to me knowing that I was living so close to my attacker. Those questions started to fill my head again: What if he comes back? What if you run into him while in the grocery store or at the mall?

Fear still played its ugly games with me. One morning, I was getting dressed for work and, apparently, my neighbor living above me woke up and tripped over something that fell on the floor. Maybe it was a floor lamp or something but it sounded like someone was breaking into my apartment through the patio door, as loud as it was. For a second, I stood there in my bathroom frozen. I couldn't move. My heart was pounding so loud. The only thing I could think of was that John had made his way back to my place, found a way to climb on my balcony and forced his way inside. I couldn't do anything but stand there and remain locked up in the bathroom. While waiting for the next sound, I stood there clutching my cell phone and pepper spray. I had formed a habit of taking my defense weapons with me everywhere I'd go, even in the house. If I was sitting in the living room watching TV, the pair had to be right next to me. I stood there, clutching my pepper spray in total silence, not even blinking my eyes, but when I didn't hear any other noises, I realized no one was inside but me.

Most nights after my court appearance, my nephew, Ron, spent the night with me. He'd walk me out in the morning when I'd leave to go to work.

I found an available apartment in a suburban area outside of Baton Rouge that included an attached garage. There weren't that many complexes with attached garages in and around the city, to my surprise. When I met with the property agent, I explained to her what happened to me and why I needed the apartment. I was pleased that the apartment was on the second floor, but it was so much bigger than the one I currently lived in. I knew I'd have to figure out ways to adjust to it.

The moving process for me was a bit draining. It was only a year ago that I had packed up my things and loaded them into two cars and moved from Texas back to Louisiana. And now, I was doing it all over again. It took so much out of me to make the phone calls to schedule movers, to set up an electricity account and transfer my internet service among other things. My family was very concerned about where I was moving to so I had to text pictures to them to reassure them that it was a typically safe place to live. Every decision that I made affected those around me and anxiety weighed heavily on my shoulders. I felt the pressure from making so many decisions not knowing if the outcome would work in my favor.

The last day I went back to my old apartment to get the rest of my things, tears welled up in my eyes. I remembered the day I moved in and I was so excited. I had no idea, then, that nine months later, I'd walk into a battle zone that would change my life forever.

After boxing my things and loading up, I drove around to the back of the complex where the incident happened. I hadn't been around there since the day I was attacked. I stopped, took some pictures, and sat inside my vehicle for a few minutes, reminiscing. I just couldn't believe that someone tried to kill me just a few feet away. I could hardly see the parking lot because my vision was so blurred. It was almost surreal knowing that my last view of Earth could have been in that very spot. It could have been the darkest moment in my life. I could have taken my last breath alone in the dark without family and friends surrounding me.

Because my new apartment was so much bigger, it took some time for me to get used to it. I was grateful for the attached garage and that I didn't have to go outside in the mornings to go to work but when night fell, I still had that odd, uncomfortable feeling. I had to form new coping skills in order to feel comfortable living and sleeping there. Because there was a door that connected my bedroom and bathroom together, I'd lock my bedroom and bathroom door so I could sleep comfortably leaving the connecting door open in between. And I'd leave my closet door cracked open with the light on because I still couldn't sleep in total darkness. The apartment was too big for me to play the one TV I had all night from my living room, so I decided to put my CD player in the bed with me and listen to sermons. I'd make sure to press the repeat button before I fell asleep otherwise I was sure to wake up some time during the night wondering why it was so quiet. It actually happened to me once and the moment I opened my eyes I got this frightening feeling in the pit of my stomach. My number one rule was to never turn on lights from my ceiling. I felt too exposed. If there was someone watching me or stalking me, I wanted to make sure that they couldn't track my steps so easily.

Once I got settled in, I thought my life would get back to the way things used to be, but it didn't. Work wasn't going so well for me either. I guess I thought staying busy every day would put me back into a normal state of mind, but I was wrong. Sometimes, it took all I had to roll out of bed and make my final destination to the chair that stood in front of my desk. It was a struggle. At any time, I'd get so emotional, you'd think I was pregnant. I tried to hide it as much as possible to keep from being noticed by those around me. I was very withdrawn and sometimes, I'd sit at my desk all day saying very few words with my headphone on in one ear listening to music. I figured if I focused on my daily work, I'd shove those thoughts of what happened to me out of my head. But, nothing worked. There wasn't an easy answer to fix this. I just wanted it to all go away.

One day, while sitting at my desk, I got a phone call from a friend I worked with at a previous job. She found out that one of our co-workers committed suicide a few weeks prior. I didn't realize that getting devastating news like that would trigger my emotions and send them into a whirlwind, but it did. I think I got so upset because it was such a sudden blow. It came out of nowhere. I wasn't prepared to handle it. Dealing with my own trauma and then hearing about a suicide of someone else took me to another level. Many of us knew that he had some issues with depression and things of that nature, but I never thought he'd take it that far. I didn't know how to cope with the decision he made at this unstable stage in my own life. I didn't know when I'd get more shocking news about something I couldn't handle. I realized that I didn't have my emotions under control at all.

I needed to talk to someone, and I needed to get some help. I wasn't concerned with the stigma people had placed upon those who decided to attend counseling and talk to a therapist. I didn't care if someone thought I was crazy or out of my mind, I was desperate. I needed someone who I thought could help me put some of these emotions to rest and fix this. In my own ignorance, I thought this was the answer.

To my surprise, it took a moment for me to find the right therapist. I didn't realize I was going to have to work that hard to seek out what I needed. I knew I wanted a female therapist because there was no way I was going to sit across from a male in a closed-in office after what happened to me. And I knew I needed someone who had worked with victims before but a lot of therapist that advertised online didn't include their picture, and for me that was a major priority. By looking into their face, I needed confirmation that I could at least sit across from them even if I wasn't ready to trust them just yet. Finally, a few days later, I contacted one who I thought met my needs and I made an appointment to see her.

I was a little nervous on my first visit. I noticed as I approached the building that my therapist and those she shared an office with didn't display an advertisement on the main door entrance that this was a therapy office for patients. Even though it didn't really bother me, it made me feel a little more relaxed knowing that they were there to make the patients feel as comfortable as possible. Sometimes people don't want others to know that they are seeking professional help and I guess it's good when they can keep things under the radar and obtain a low profile.

I liked that my appointment was scheduled after work because it didn't interfere with my work schedule. And, I didn't have to worry about anyone questioning why I was leaving work early or what kind of doctor's appointment I had. Although I didn't care if anyone knew that I was going to counseling, I just didn't want people knowing the ins and outs of when I go and how long I stayed. I wanted to keep that part of my life very private.

I arrived a little early and sat out in the lobby, waiting. There were no other patients in the waiting area but me. It was a cozy room with a couch and several chairs. A hallway ran along the back with several offices used by other thera- pists. Soft music played and I could smell the scent of some sort of aroma in the air.

A tall man and a tiny little lady exited an office that sat across from the lobby. The man passed by me on his way out the door. The lady came and introduced herself, and handed me some documents to read over. A few minutes later, she in- vited me into her office. A two-seat couch sat along the wall and a little table stood in the center of the floor. Across from the table was her desk where she kept books and notepads and would sometimes take notes as I talked. I noticed a box of Kleenex sat in the center of the table and I saw a few toys laying around apparently for children that she counseled. She explained to me some of the guidelines and that she wasn't allowed to discuss anything I said with anyone else. But she did stress that if I mentioned anything about harm- ing myself, harming someone else or that an elderly person or child was being abused, she'd have to report it. When she finished, I signed the documents, and then we got started.

I told her what happened. How I became a victim of a crime, giving her every detail I remembered, but I didn't open up very much about my feelings. I really didn't know how far to go. Maybe it was because I didn't trust her or I wanted to keep my emotions under control. Granted, I didn't want her to think that I was completely unstable where I couldn't function at all. I wanted her to think that I had some control. Maybe I was trying to impress her; I don't really know. Basically, we just touched the surface in most areas during our first session. She asked me if I wanted to come back and I told her yes. Leaving her office that day, I didn't feel like anything had changed. To be honest, I guess I thought that in one session all of those negative emotions would be sucked out of my life. But that didn't happen. I think I was expecting something that I didn't get. Perhaps, a quick fix. Over the course of this storm, I had to learn that healing is a process and it takes time. There are no quick fixes and only God and time can close a wound. But I knew at that moment that I needed to give this a chance and that maybe this could work; it could at least put me on the right road to freedom.

I began to open up more over the next several weeks as things in my life unfolded. I talked about my issue of being angry because this happened to me, of being withdrawn, of dealing with fear, and of feeling ignored by a judicial system that didn't always properly work in favor of good citizens. There were times when my emotions bubbled over and she saw my tears. She saw how frustrated I was when my court dates continued over and over again and how people around me didn't understand what I was going through and how they were very critical of me. So much was said that she saw all of me. She saw me as a broken victim and a strong survivor. She never provided a solution to my problems but sometimes would ask questions on top of questions to draw me in deeper. Sometimes, we talked about things that I had never discussed with anyone else before in my life, those deep things that I kept hidden, afraid to expose. I often felt sorry for her because it became common for me to allow my thoughts to build up over the week and then let it all out in my sessions. But I had so much weight on my shoulders that I just needed to unload. I knew that she was getting a handful every single time I arrived. But, she was attentive, and maybe that is what I needed. Just someone to listen.

CHAPTER 17

Brick Walls

⟿

Looking unto Jesus the author and finisher
of our faith; who for the joy that was set
before him endured the cross, despising the
shame, and is set down at the right hand
of the throne of God. (Hebrews 12:2)

I WAS SCHEDULED FOR ANOTHER court date after the first of the year in early January. The prosecutor wasn't sure if my case would be heard because, apparently, John's psychiatric evaluation wasn't requested and she told me not to attend but to be on standby. She called me that afternoon and told me they had rescheduled the court date for the end of the month.

At the end of January during the next court appearance, my sisters drove into town to be with me. They got to see my new place and was pleased. Although they didn't come out and say it, I figured they were glad when I made the decision to move out of the apartment where I was assaulted. I know they were probably able to rest better knowing that I was no longer there and I wouldn't have to go outside in the mornings to go to work. But for me, it was hard making decisions. I felt like I had made so many mistakes in the decisions I made leading up my incident that I was stressed and afraid that I'd make yet another bad one. Almost everything I did and the decisions I made had an effect on my entire family because they wanted to make sure that I was safe and okay.

The judge I stood before during the initial court hearing term ended and was not re-elected, so a new judge was placed into office and took over my case. The defense attorney asked that the case be continued again because the psychiatric evaluation wasn't complete, and he wanted to request another therapist to conduct the evaluation. I assumed he thought that by choosing his own therapist and asking the new judge for permission would work in his favor. Sure enough, the judge granted his request.

Every time I attended court and saw John, I noticed that I started to have symptoms like I did after I was attacked. It felt like someone was always coming up behind me, especially at night.

I remember standing in front of the bathroom mirror, telling myself that no one was inside the house but me. I would pray aloud, trying to put pressure on fear to leave me alone. I wasn't going to let him control or take over me. It just wasn't going to happen. I had come too far and I wasn't giving up on me!

In February at the next hearing, the defense asked for another continuation. He said that one of the guardians couldn't make it and asked the judge if it could be continued again. This time, I was aware of the game he was playing. He figured that if he could push me to the limit, I'd get tired and give up. It seemed to aggravate him every single time he'd look back in the courtroom and see me and my family sitting there. Evidently, the presence of my family and I meant everything. Even when my sisters couldn't make it, my parents and my brother and I were always there. We weren't giving up. The prosecutor told me when I initially met with her that some victims never show up for court. They walk away with so much pain, and a juvenile who needs to be put away walks back out onto the streets. But, I was determined to see this to the bitter end. I had been through too much to give up now.

The defense attorney even tried to convince the judge that I didn't have to be present at the sentencing. I was shocked at the words that came out of his mouth. He knew that if I wasn't at the sentencing, I wouldn't have the opportunity to testify and for some reason he must have assumed that my words would have a powerful effect on this case. I was going to be there just like I was there the morning John stabbed me. Hopefully, I was going to see him chained and locked away. I wasn't going to miss that for the world because it would validate my ability to move on with at least that part of my life.

The judge apologized to me when he granted the defense another continuation but did state that this case had been lingering way too long. He thought it was senseless. He promised me that my case would be the first one he reviewed at the next court appearance. He asked me to give him a specific time as to when I wanted him to review the case. He said that if I said I wanted it reviewed at 9:07 a.m., then 9:07 a.m. it would be. Sitting in my pew, I told him that I was tired of dealing with all of this. I couldn't understand how a case could be continued for months and months to no end. None of it made sense to me. I was so aggravated but I had no other choice but to trust him. He was a new judge that the citizens had put into office, and I was counting on him to stand on the promises he made to this community and do something about this kid.

I still attended counseling every week or every other week. Each time I'd attend, my therapist gave me something to read or additional information to look up on the Internet. While I sat in session one Friday evening, she told me that even though I didn't die in the attack, I was grieving. I was surprised because I had no idea that my incident was associated with grief, but I remembered writing in one of my blogs that I felt like a part of me died. She went over the five stages of grief with me and told me that they could appear in no certain order. I was relieved because it brought some clarity as to why I was doing some of the things I was doing.

I woke up that Saturday morning, got online, and read about grief in detail. As I read about the five stages, things started to make sense. I started to understand why I was doing certain things or feeling a certain way. I felt a sense of liberation because now I understood why I was blaming myself, withdrawn, angry, depressed, and isolated. Yes, all these things were normal for a person dealing with grief. I wasn't crazy or unstable or out of control; this was something that everybody dealt with whether they were a crime victim or had lost a loved one or went through a bad breakup or divorce. This instantly changed my perspective on my situation. Maybe I was progressing after all. Or, maybe I was dealing with all of this in a normal way. But so many times, I felt like I wasn't. I felt so abnormal because it seemed like everybody else who had been through something just wiped away their tears and picked back up where they left off. I got the impression that they weren't emotional like I was or depressed or angry. They were strong and resilient, not broken and shattered. They were never defeated and they never allowed anything to ever get next to them. But I had to believe that maybe that wasn't the truth. Maybe, they seized their storm in a state of denial and maybe they still hadn't healed. I don't know. I was just relieved to know that I had found some answers that I was looking for. And, knowing this gave me so much clarity.

I felt pretty good that day. That was probably the first time I felt normal in a long time. It was almost like I had my old life back. With an array of hope, I was smiling and feeling confident that this was going to work out and things were going to get better. Feeling good in my spirit, as if I had accomplished something, I decided to go out and run some errands. It was a beautiful day with nice weather, and nothing could have been better than me getting out of the house to get some sunshine.

For some reason I don't remember, I had to go to a specific store in south Baton Rouge that day, so I decided to run all my errands in that area. On my way home, I made one last stop and pulled into an empty parking space at a department store. It was early afternoon so shoppers were out everywhere. As I stepped out of my vehicle and started walking toward the store, I noticed John's guardians on the next aisle over walking to their car. He wasn't with them and they didn't see me, but it was such a weird feeling. At that split moment, I couldn't make up my mind what I should. Should I go back to the truck and leave? Or, should I hurry inside the store? Definitely, I didn't want them to see me and thank God they didn't. That moment brought back every memory I had of him, and I got really nervous. Because we weren't confined to a small courtroom with security officers around, I felt unprotected. I had no one to shelter me if something happened. As they pulled away, I hurried inside the store. I didn't know what to do so I texted my sisters. Jean called me immediately to see if I was okay. I led her to believe that I was fine, but I really wasn't. For a moment, the tears came and then fear paid a visit, and I started to frequently look behind me assuming someone was coming upon me. I was very jumpy expecting something to happen. What if they came back in the store, I thought? What was I going to do? What if they approached me? What would I say? As I stood in one of the aisles, all those thoughts played a part in my head. Browsing shoppers, who had no idea what was going on with me, would quietly walk up behind me looking for an item I was standing next to and it would frighten me. I felt like everybody in that busy store was out to get me and in my mind they were all suspects. I didn't trust anyone. I didn't know if someone was going to quickly run up behind me and harm me or what. I couldn't concentrate on what I needed to get, and I was so uncomfortable that I just left my shopping cart in the middle of the aisle and went home.

The remainder of my weekend was an emotional roller-coaster ride. Just seeing them in public, outside the courtroom, triggered everything. I never thought that I would run into them since I had moved to a community outside the city, and I didn't have a plan as to how I would handle that. With my emotions and fear, I felt like I was back at square one. Every time it seemed like I was moving forward in this fight, I'd get knocked down again. It hadn't been four hours since I had read an article about grief and felt I like I was getting somewhere with all of this before

I ran smack into a red brick wall. I questioned and wondered how long I would have to endure this agony. How long would I have to ride on this rollercoaster? When was it going to stop? When was I going to be able to get off? It was merely tormenting. I was exhausted and I desperately needed some relief.

CHAPTER 18

Tribulations

&

These things I have spoken unto you, that
in me ye might have peace. In the world ye
shall have tribulations: but be of good cheer;
I have overcome the world. (John 16:33)

Before going through this test and trial, I would have thought that my tribulation would have been the attack I was involved in a little over five months ago, but it is actually all the aftermath that comes because of it. I've come to learn that the tribulation wasn't during the few seconds it took my attacker to stab me, but it is all the things that unfolded afterward. It is dealing with rebuilding my life from the ground up, learning to live again and trying to figure out who I am. It is dealing with fear and fighting the spirit of fear that wants to keep me bound. It is the medical bills that I am now receiving, the money I've spent to try and find somewhere that I think is potentially a safer place to live while paying deposits and movers, and the increase in my monthly budget.

My tribulation is dealing with people who don't under-stand me, who judge me and say it doesn't take all that to get over something like this—who look me in the eye and say that I should handle this the same way I've handled everything else that has come my way. People have no idea what it is like to live this way, to get up every morning fighting for some-thing that has been taken away. One thing I've learned about people is that they don't have the patience to allow God to heal the broken. I wonder if they could walk in my shoes for just one day. There is no instruction book that tells you how to go about dealing with something of this magnitude. Sometimes, they remind me of my attacker who has no remorse for what he did to me, who shows no emotions at all. They would probably declare from the mountaintop that they are nothing like him but the fruit that they bear says something far different.

Blog Post: "The Tribulation"

THERE WAS A MAN WHO came to work one morning and started eating a bagel for breakfast. He either choked on it or incurred a coughing spell because he started cough-ing a lot. It was so bad that everyone could hear him and someone asked him if he was okay and if he needed some water. He couldn't answer but nodded his head. He coughed uncontrollably for what seemed like an entire minute. Some people around him empathized with him with whispers of concern because he couldn't seem to catch his breath.

For a few seconds or so, he stopped, but then started right back up again in full force. While some had expressed their concern, other people around him started to get aggravated. You could hear it in the comments they were making. In an obnoxiously joking way, one person stood up to a small group of people who sat around him and said "If he's a smoker, he needs to stop smoking all of those cigarettes" while his audience sniggered in agreement.

Through this entire ordeal, no one had the patience to allow this man to get it together. Their empathy and concern quickly faded away. Why? Because it was an inconvenience to them. They didn't want to be bothered with hearing him cough. From the comments they made, he either needed to drink some water to resolve the issue or get up and go outside. But, even if the situation wasn't handled outside, I don't think they really cared. They just wanted him out of their presence because he was making their lives uncomfortable.

I have learned that when you are going through a storm in life, people do not have the patience to allow you to heal. They will show you empathy for a moment and when it's gone, it's gone. If you haven't gotten over your ordeal within the time restraints that they think you should, empathy on their part has been flushed down the drain.

Many times, I'd discuss this with my therapist. Once, she told me that I had a mild form of PTSD (Post Traumatic Stress Disorder), but it wasn't anything severe. I remember someone asking me one day when was I going to start working out. Without any knowledge of what PTSD meant, they assumed that working out would relieve my stress and cure my problem. I mean literally, cure my problem. I laughed as I sat with her telling this story while she looked at me with a blank expression. I told her that if every soldier who came home from war with PTSD would just sign a contract with 24Hour Fitness, all their troubles would be over. It didn't matter how many times they closed their eyes and saw dead bodies or heard bombs exploding or had a flashback, working out would cure it all.

But, it isn't that simple. Yes, working out plays a vivid role in relieving stress, but it doesn't cure PTSD. A person's mental capacity in conjunction with other things sums up what PTSD is, and a lot of people don't understand that.

The bottom line is that it takes time to heal. There are no quick fixes. Sometimes, your body and mind are in such a state of shock that it takes months to process things and release. It isn't something that happens overnight. But, we live in such an instant society where everything is available at the tip of our fingers and nobody wants to wait for anything. Everything is so microwavable and if patience has to be exercised, it can become a problem.

The story that I told you at the beginning of this chapter reminds me so much of the Bible story of Job. Job was a God-fearing man who was very wealthy, but he lost almost everything he had: houses, cattle, servants, and even his children. If that wasn't enough, he became very ill until boils pierced his body. His friends came to his aid and sat with him for an entire week without saying a word. But, what was so disturbing was what came out of their mouths when they did speak. They concluded that surely he had done something wrong to deserve all of it. Can you imagine the conversation they had on their way to visit Job? They even tried to force him to admit to his wrongdoings. Surely, there was no one as righteous as Job, they said. There was no way that God would favor such a man.

But, Job fought back. Even while grieving the loss of his children, the loss of his finances, and the sickness that came upon his body, Job always had a comeback word. He stood his ground. And, no matter what they said, he'd make a proclamation to be heard. He nearly demanded it. And, every single time, he'd say that he wasn't guilty of any wrongdoing. But perhaps Job was speaking out of his emotions. Obviously being in his state of mind, his emotions were at an all-time high. He had been through a lot and so much had already been snatched away from him that he wasn't going to allow them to take away his dignity too. It was the only thing he had left that was of value and I believe he would have fought to the bitter end to hold on to it. Being in a similar situation as Job, I liked that he fought back and stood his ground but I questioned was it really worth it? Was it worth him standing up in the face of his critics? Was it worth him running around trying to convince everybody that the lies that were being spread about him weren't true? Or, trying to prevent the gossip from reaching an all-time high? Was he really going to benefit from running around, wasting his time, spinning his wheels? No matter how much Job explained that he did nothing wrong, they were going to believe what they wanted to believe about him whether it was true or not. And although Job allowed his emotions to get the best of him, in the end God still instructed him to forgive them, and God allowed those who criticized him to turn around and bless him with twice as much as he had before.

I have learned that in some storms, you have to wave against the war of the opinion of others. It seems that while you're in the eye of your storm, that is when you are judged the most. If they aren't trying to give you a play-by-play of how you should get over something quickly, healed or not healed, they're telling you why you're going through the challenge. They are reminding you of the things they think you did that caused these winds to blow your way. They're telling you what you should have done or how you could have avoided this in the first place.

An opinion is just what it is…one's judgment on a particular thought. It doesn't mean that it is truth or concrete information. It is only a person's point of view. It is how they view things or see things from their own perspective. Many times opinions derive from people who have never been a victim before such as myself. They are simply stating their point of view from a non-violent, non-victim standpoint. They may be giving their thoughts on something that they have never experienced before in their lives. It is merely their judgment call on an idea of how they think something should occur. I think when a survivor understands this entire concept it can cause a positive shift in the mind-set and their healing process can remain constant and intact without distractions, otherwise it can deter them from healing. It can cause them to become bitter and angry because at the peak of a storm a person's emotions are highly sensitive and the distractions and opinions of others are extremely magnified. The key for me was staying centered in Christ and finding comfort in Him. I had to constantly go back to His word and be reminded of who He said that I was. I couldn't allow the opinions of others to define who I was even if many of them believed it. I had to know who I was in Christ and stand on that.

CHAPTER 19

Friday the 13th

‿⎯

But the Lord said unto me, Say not, I am a child:
for thou shalt go to all that I shall send thee, and
whatsoever I command thee thou shalt speak.
Then the Lord put forth his hand, and touched my
mouth. And the Lord said unto me, Behold, I have
put my words in thy mouth. (Jeremiah 1: 7, 9)

I remember once, in one of my therapy sessions, my therapist shared with me something called the Hero's Road. She talked about how we go through life on this winding road and we fight everything that comes against us. When we return to our place of familiarity, we find purpose and share with others our experiences. I believe that I have been on that Hero's Road for the past six months. And, with God's help, I believe that I have been transformed from a victim to a victor. Although I may not be fully there, I still speak it in faith. I believe that it is now time for me to share my story and help other victims reach their destination of victory. I believe that my purpose is to allow God to use my hands, my feet, my mouth, my eyes, and my ears to help Him transform others into victors—to encourage them along the way—to help them overcome whatever it is that they are going through in their lives for the kingdom of God.

So, I celebrate today because I am no longer a victim but I am a victor. I am a winner. I am more than a conqueror through Jesus Christ. I share my victory dance because I believe that this is my season of plenty. It is my season to have joy, gladness, thanksgiving, and melodies (Isaiah 51:3). This is my season of sunshine in Jesus' name. Amen!

Blog Post: "From Victim to Victor"

FRIDAY, MARCH 13, 2015. IT rained so hard on the day of sentencing that when we got out of the car and walked into the building, puddles of water were everywhere. Everybody carried umbrellas to keep from getting soaking wet.

I had received a call about two weeks prior that John's guardians went before the court and had him placed into state custody because he threatened to harm them. Apparently, a confrontation occurred in the home and he promised that he would do to them what he did to me, and they had him removed from the home. I was in total shock.

I believed he had become so comfortable with the fact that he hadn't been sentenced that he felt liberated enough to strike again. I believed he thought nothing would come of this and he would walk free.

So, this time, when he entered the courtroom, he wore an orange jumpsuit and chains. He sat next to the defense attorney and his guardians; however, I didn't see any form of communication or fellowship between him and his guardians at all. As I observed, I don't recall them even saying one word to him.

Just as the judge promised, my case was the first one to be heard. A while back, I had been informed by the prosecutor that I would have to testify that day and tell my story to place more weight on the case. As I approached the sentencing date, I asked God to give me the right words to say. I wanted my words to be effective and have an impact on the hearts of the decision makers. As God reminded me of things that were said and discussed at the initial hearing, I played those thoughts over and over in my mind until I had outlined what I would say.

The defense attorney once again tried to ask for a continuation. This time he stated that he had spoken with John's grandmother who wanted to make arraignments to come and pick the boy up, and move him back to Texas with her. Obviously in some way, she could do that but she had to give her employer a two-week notice that she needed to take off and attend court. I thought to myself, why would anyone want a child in their home that was threatening to take the lives of people who were trying to take care of him? Not only did he try to take my life, but he threatened his guardians who had provided a roof over his head and food to eat. What made her think that he wouldn't do the same thing to her? And when he approached her with a knife, how was she going to handle that? She knew well in advance that this kid was going to be sentenced, but like him, maybe she thought that nothing was going to come of this case. And now, she wanted to take him back with her. Evidently she realized that the young couple didn't want to have any more dealings with him and they wanted him off of their hands in one way or the other. I really don't know what was going on inside that family but we all could tell that there was trouble brewing. When the defense announced his request, the judge looked straight at me. I started to shake my head from side to side. I wasn't dealing with this any longer. There was no way that I was going to go through this another day. I came mentally prepared; this was going to be the last time I stepped foot inside the courtroom. The judge denied his request. The defense attorney said that he did his part by asking and he'd have to tell the grandmother that the court denied her request.

When I took the stand, I didn't even look at John. I had decided that this day was not going to be about him. He would not be glorified at all for what he did to me. My focus was to say what I thought should happen to him, how this incident had changed my life, and what I planned to do going forward.

The prosecutor guided me through some questions at times but at other times, she allowed my thoughts to flow. I started off by sharing what happened. Then, I stressed the fact that I felt he needed to receive the maximum sentence because his intent was to take my life. No one in their right mind would approach another individual so that they could identify them, described what they looked like and what they were wearing if their intent wasn't to kill them. I said that I specifically remember him stating on record the day he took the plea that I scared him when I jumped up after him. He thought that when I fell I wasn't going to get up. He assumed that he had completed his mission and killed me. The defense attorney shook his head when I made that statement because he knew that I had set a trap. He knew that the judge would have to consider John's intent in all of this. It wasn't a matter of if he did it, John had already made that clear. It was a matter of John having the victory in killing me. I glanced over at him and noticed him staring at me as if he was hearing this story for the first time. It was almost as if he was taking mental notes as to what not to do the next time around to get away with murder. He was very disturbing to me. He showed no form of guilt or remorse at all. I then shared how the incident had changed my life, how he took something away from me that I would never get back. I talked about how I was trying to get my life back on track and although it had been tough, I was determined to fight and win. But, my main focus was to share how I wanted to help other victims in some way. Deep down inside I had a desire to share my experiences with others who were going through the same thing. No one could understand this awful pain but another victim who had been violated and brutally assaulted in some way. Even if they felt isolated, I wanted them to know that they were not alone. I wanted them to know that there are others out there dealing with the same issues. And just maybe in some way, sharing my story with them would help me heal too.

Before I left the stand, the court asked John if he would like to say anything to me and he said no. Unfortunately, he had no desire to apologize to me at all and I was okay with that. I could clearly see that he was too immature to understand the damage he had caused me. I didn't go to court that day expecting him to have an epiphany at all. He had a lot of learning to do. And I felt that if he did this because he felt it was his desire to show himself as a man or prove to be domineering or controlling in some way, I knew that hopefully where he was going someone would be just as angry if not angrier and put him in his rightful place.

In closing statements, the defense attorney tried to convince the judge that John didn't need the maximum sentence. He said maybe he needed to serve a little time but he didn't feel like he deserved to serve a full sentence. Grant it, John had turned 15 since the attack and that would only give him 6 years in the detention center. To me, that really wasn't enough. I felt that he should serve more than that. But I guess to the defense it just wasn't that serious but to me it was my life that John tried to take. The prosecutor in return highly stressed that John was definitely a threat to society. If his intentions were to harm his guardians, the people who took care of him and sheltered him, surely he wouldn't have a problem harming anyone else if he was allowed the opportunity. She pulled everything she could out of the bag to make this case work in our favor.

I held my breath when the judge made his ruling. I was pretty confident that the words I said along with my prosecutor's closing statement went in my favor, and thank God they did. The judge talked about how this was a senseless, brutal, and violent crime. He couldn't understand why he wasn't charged as an adult from the beginning. He had no other choice but to give John the maximum sentence. He was going to have to serve time and stay locked behind bars until he turned 21. And because of some other things discussed in court regarding his psychiatric evaluation, he requested that John be held in solitary confinement.

This time, when John left the courtroom, he didn't scan my row and look for me. I don't think he was pleased with the results. I think he got a little too comfortable assuming things would work in his favor. Maybe he thought that his grandmother was going to come and rescue him and he'd tell Louisiana goodbye for good. But, God will always prevail for His children, those who love and trust Him. Although it felt like it took an eternity to get to an end result, God was working in my favor and He came through for me. Had it not been for all of the continued court dates, my case may not have been viewed by the new judge who had been recently elected and made a promise to the community to change how these juveniles were being sentenced. I realized that patience is a virtue and sometimes we don't always know what God is doing but stepping back and allowing Him to take full control is the key.

Tears filled my eyes when I stood up to leave the room. It was finally over. I could finally move on with at least this part of my journey. I shook hands with my prosecutor's boss, who stood by her side as they handled my case. People who sat around us in court congratulated me, saying that they were going to keep us in prayer. When I walked out of the courtroom, my niece, Jada, gave me a hug and told me that everything was going to be okay. And surprisingly, the defense attorney approached me and told me that he was sorry that this happened to me. Even then, I wasn't angry at him because I knew that he was just trying to do his job. I had learned while dealing with the justice system that staying angry wasn't the answer. I had too much to lose by staying in a state of anger. I had a life to live and I wanted to make the best of it however I could.

This was a huge weight off my shoulders. Even though tears welled up in my eyes, I smiled inside because God had answered my prayers by touching the hearts of those in the judicial system. I also smiled because my family and I did it. We got through this part of the test and I was so grateful. It had been a long road, but we came out victorious.

Before leaving, my family and I met back in the conference room with the prosecutor and her boss when court recessed. We talked about the case and a few things she wanted me to know. They also told me of a support group they were getting ready to start that they wanted me to be a part of. They said that someone was going to call me within a few days.

Before we left, we thanked the prosecutor and her boss for the wonderful job they did in helping us. We thanked them for their patience and kindness and loving their job enough to care about people.

My family and I went out to lunch after court. They had fallen in love with a restaurant not far from my apartment. On court dates, I never had to ask where we were going to eat; I always knew. After lunch, they all piled inside my apartment and we sat around and talked. My mom, sisters, nieces, and I were all inside hanging out while my brother was on the balcony cutting his son's and my dad's hair. It was like old times.

Later on, I stood out on the balcony with my sisters, and I looked up and saw the sun peeking through the clouds. The rain had stopped and the sun was aggressively pushing its way through. I thought about it for a moment and knew that God was speaking to me. Just like He told Noah through the sign of the rainbow that there would never be another flood, I knew that He was telling me that although I had been through the storm and the heavy rain, He promised that the sun was going to shine again in my life. And, I still stand on that promise today.

My brother and parents left that Friday evening to go back home, but my sisters stayed for the weekend. They left early Sunday morning to go back to Texas. They didn't know it and I didn't tell them, but I cried that day. It was a bittersweet moment. I enjoyed the frequent visits from them but I knew that everyone had to go back to living their lives, and we probably wouldn't see each other as often.

Now that we are older, they are more like three best friends to me than sisters. Although we disagree and argue sometimes, we always make our way back to each other somehow. Each one of them give me something totally different that I need.

I didn't go to work that Monday. I took the day off and rested. I was so mentally drained and my wound ached really bad, probably from having anxiety for such a long period of time and worrying about what the outcome of the sentencing would be. I could tell that my muscles were trying to relax from of the tension that had built up in my body. I was so tired that I think I stayed in bed probably until almost noon that day resting.

CHAPTER 20

Moving On

*So that thou incline thine ear unto wisdom,
and apply thine heart to understanding; Yea, if
thou criest after knowledge, and liftest up thy
voice for understanding. (Proverbs 2: 2-3)*

ABOUT THREE WEEKS LATER, JUST like my prosecutor
promised, I got a call from someone at the East Baton
Rouge Parish District Attorney's Office regarding the support group. She told me that they were going to start the
program within the next week. I was excited to attend because I wanted to get as much help as possible and I was
anxious to finally meet someone like me, someone who
had gone through a traumatic experience too.

We met every Thursday for an hour and a half. For
the first four weeks, no one showed up but me and the
two therapists who had been assigned to facilitate the
group. No other victims would come out and join. When

the facilitators would call and leave messages, some would never return the call, others made excuses that the time slot wasn't a good fit for them and a few promised to come but never showed up. I guess they just didn't want to deal with having to talk about or relive their horrible tragedy. Maybe they had buried their emotions so deep inside that it would cost too much to unravel them and bring them back to the fore front. This really bothered me. First, I couldn't understand why people didn't want to get help. How were they planning to survive and live through this? I wanted as much help as possible. Even in my ignorance of thinking that this support group could possibly be the answer and take away some of my pain, I came anyway looking for something that I didn't find. But, I came. This entire ordeal that I was experiencing caused me to wonder how were people who had been victims dealing with their assaults. Maybe they had suppressed their pain so deep inside that they found their crutch, something to lean on to temporarily take away their pain. Perhaps their crutch came in the form of violence or substance abuse or some sort of addiction. I really don't know. I just knew that this was way too much for me to try and figure it all out. Second, I couldn't understand why there wasn't a support group already in place for assault victims. Yes, there were resources for rape and domestic violence victims because I had researched that information online a few days after I was attacked. But I was unable to find anything for those who had been stabbed, robbed or held at gunpoint. Yet, it was 2015 and violent, brutal, crimes were being committed every single day. You could clearly see the manifestation of it by watching the evening news. Luckily I had health insurance with my employer and was able to go to counseling but I wondered about all of the others who didn't have that privilege. I wondered about those who never sought out counseling or spoke up in court and said they wanted to get help or help somebody else. Sometimes people who are fearful or afraid or who don't really understand the importance of counseling just need a little tug or someone to hold their hand and lead the way. But in this situation, there was nothing to lead them to.

I could sense that every time I showed up and no one else came, the therapists were getting anxious because you really can't have a support group without more than one victim. Although they didn't allow me to, I volunteered and asked if I could call some of the survivors myself to convince them to come out to a session. I wanted them to know that I was just like them. I had been angry and depressed and fearful too, and we all needed help. I was eager to hear their stories and learn from them. I had anticipated finally finding somebody else who was just like me.

One day, a gentleman walked in. I was told that he was going to attend the next week and I was excited about it because we could finally get started. But, it caught me off guard when they told me that I would be sitting across the table from a male victim. I was so wrapped up in my emotions of how I was dealing with my own assault that I never thought about how male victims deal with trauma and assault. I asked the facilitators about that and they told me that usually male victims are very angry. They internalize things and aren't emotional like some female victims.

I was anxious but a little nervous the day he arrived. I was eager to hear what he had to say and possibly learn something from him. When he introduced himself and started to speak, I realized that although we were both of different ethnicities and backgrounds we had so much in common. He was an elderly man who had been robbed and shot at gunpoint. About six years prior, his van ran hot one New Year's Day and he pulled over to a gas station to let it cool when two young juveniles drove up. One got out of the car and walked over to him and asked to use his cell phone. He told the young man that he would make the call for him which turned out to be a bogus number. When the young man insisted on using his phone and the man refused, he then pulled out a gun and shot him. He fought back but sustained two gunshot wounds in the leg. He talked about his battle with depression, anger, fear, and criticism. There was such a connection that it was unreal because I was dealing with the same things. I understood his pain and his frustration. I understood what it was like for him to be judged while trying to figure out how to put his life back together again. Although our incidents were far different, our struggle was parallel. We were walking down the same path trying to figure it all out.

They decided to name the support group "Moving Into the Light," and it reminded me so much of the final sentencing day and how the sunshine pushed through the clouds after the rain. I could concur that I did move into the light with all the information they provided and the things they taught us. They gave us homework assignments, and I learned about coping skills, how to deal with uncertainties, breathing techniques, flashbacks, and triggers, among other things. I almost felt like I was going to school. I thought we would spend an hour and a half talking about our incidents but I had no idea that I would be taken down a road that filled me with so much knowledge of what it really meant to be a victim and how to survive. As they went over lesson after lesson each week, I saw myself in each one of them.

One of my most memorable moments I think is when I learned about flashbacks and that it isn't always bad to have them. When you go through a traumatic experience, your body records the information through your five senses, and that is why smells or the touch of something can trigger your thoughts back to the incident. But, a flashback is when your body is sending the information, the trauma, to your brain to record it. During the flashback, something will trigger and your thoughts will go back to the incident but your body releases that particular moment in time to your brain. And, your brain is ready to receive and store that experience somewhere. It releases the trauma from your body and in my opinion puts less pressure, stress, or anxiety on it. The positive thing about a flashback is that it is a form of healing because, in some cases, the flashbacks become less frequent as the memories are being stored in the brain.

I had no idea that this was how flashbacks worked and what it really meant to have one. I remember telling the facilitators that I had a flashback one day and for days, I beat myself up thinking that I just wasn't healing and I couldn't understand why. It had been months since my incident and I felt like I shouldn't have been feeling that way. I blamed myself for something I didn't understand. I thought that having a flashback was holding me back instead of pushing me forward.

I remember that day so well. I got dressed for work that morning and I turned off my CD player in my bathroom and went into the kitchen to fix breakfast. I have no idea why I decided to turn it off because I always listened to music or a sermon at that time of the morning to occupy my mind. When I went into the kitchen, there was such a stillness— dead silence all around. It seemed like the entire apartment complex was on lockdown in a quiet mode. I didn't hear any cars passing by or anything. It was dark and dead silence surrounded me just like the morning that I was attacked. All of sudden while standing in the kitchen, I went back in time and I heard myself screaming. It was that same desperate cry, pleading for someone to help me. For some reason, I couldn't get it out of my head for the few seconds it occurred. When I came to myself, I was crying and couldn't understand why no one aided me when they heard me screaming. There were apartments that sat all around me in close proximity and no one came to rescue me. I know that someone was up getting dressed for work and they had to have heard me screaming to the top of my lungs but no one ran outside and did anything to help save my life.

I barely made it to work that day. I should have stayed home, but I knew that it wouldn't stop the thoughts in my head. I figured I'd be okay. My eyes were so blurred sitting at my desk that I decided to go to the bathroom. I stood in the stall pressuring myself to get it together. I kept trying to force myself to be who society wanted me to be…healed. But I wasn't healed. I was still dealing with a lot of pain. I was still hurting and traumatized. I was trying to figure it all out. I tried to coach myself into believing that I was all better and that I was okay. I tried to tell myself that I should have been over this by now. What was wrong with me? Why couldn't I just get it together? I took a few deep breathes and tried to suppress down my emotions and convince myself that I was okay. I thought I was ready to walk out the door and go back to my desk. When I got ready to exit, a lady walked into the bathroom, took one look at me and said something like "everything is going to be alright." When she said those words, I allowed the door I was supposed to walk out of to close in front of me and I just stood there in the middle of the floor and broke down. It was one of those moments when I just couldn't hide it. There was nowhere for me to run and hide to deal with this one in secret.

I can remember at other times when I felt that way, about to explode, I'd walk quickly to my vehicle or make it to the bathroom stall just in time so that no one would see me. I was already being judged by impatient people who wanted me to just get over it, and I didn't want them to see me having yet another setback. It would have given them that much more to talk about.

Had I known what a flashback really was, I could have handled my situation in a different way. I could have looked at it from a totally different perspective. I had been through so much already. Having dealt with fear, going back to the apartment, relocating to another one, going to counseling, and all the continued court dates, I felt like I was back at square one . . . again. But I shouldn't have. I should have been celebrating the fact that this trauma was being released from my body and being stored somewhere in my brain. And maybe, I wouldn't be so stressed or have so much anxiety. It was a milestone and I didn't even know it. Proverbs 4:7 says "Wisdom is the principal thing; therefore get wisdom: and with all thy getting get understanding." Not having the knowledge of something can nearly destroy you. You'll make decisions and come to conclusions about things based on the limited amount of information that you have. That is why I think it is so important for those who have been victims of any kind to seek help and get an understanding of what is really means to be a victim and then use the necessary tools to survive.

Week after week, my group therapy sessions were something I looked forward to. I thrived on making it my business to be there every Thursday. And, I loved the facilitators.

They made me laugh. They allowed us to be who we were, flaws and all. There was never a wrong answer to any question and if we felt angry or sad or depressed, that was okay. I loved my "partner in crime," too, because we ranted and raved about everything we didn't like and felt good about it. We laughed at each other's jokes and, yes, there were days when I cried and they saw my tears.

CHAPTER 21

Last Man Standing

—⁘—

*Yea, though I walk through the valley of
the shadow of death. (Psalm 23:4)*

AT TIMES, THE SUPPORT GROUP was the only thing that
kept me going. I didn't realize it until the group ended,
but I was thankful that I didn't join until six months after
my incident because that is when I took some really hard
blows. I was faced with some obstacles that seemed at times
almost unbearable.

I realized that I needed to take a break from work.
The company had created some new procedures that involved a lot of deadlines and quotas. They were trying
a new method to push a lot of work out that had been
stagnant for way too long. I was still dealing with a lot of
emotions from my incident and with the added pressure
from work, I didn't feel like I was progressing at all. I was
at a standstill, not moving forward. So, for my birthday,

I decided to take a few days off and visit my sisters in Dallas.

About a week before I left to go on vacation, I got a call from one of the leasing agents at my apartment saying that there was a bad water leak that occurred in my bathroom. Somehow, one of the maintenance workers saw water coming from underneath my garage or my neighbor's. They gave me the impression that it wasn't that big of a deal, but I decided to leave work anyway and check it out. When I got there, water was everywhere. It had soaked up the floor in my bathroom, bedroom, and a portion of my living room area. The leak came from a pipe near the toilet and had so much pressure behind it that the water actually reached the ceiling. Everything in my bathroom was drenched from the towels in my laundry hamper to my tissue roll—even the items that were sitting on top of my countertop around the sink. I stopped by the office to speak with the manager, and she sent one of the leasing agents out to tell me that she was in a meeting and didn't have time to talk. A few days later, when I was finally able to get her on the phone, being that she ignored my phone calls several times, she said that they were bringing in some fans to dry out the floor and the carpet for the next three days. So, I sat through three days of roaring fans constantly running throughout my apartment day and night. On day three, I called her and told her that the carpet was not dry because I could feel moisture under my feet, but she told me that she knew what she was doing.

The day I returned from my trip, I found mold growing inside my apartment. At first, it was only in the bathroom and in a small coat closet that stood between my bathroom and living room area, and also in my garage. Being that my apartment was on the second floor, one of the garage walls stood underneath the bathroom and when the leak occurred, water ran down along the garage wall. I called the manager and told her what I saw. I told her that I did not want to stay there because I didn't know how severe the damages were and I asked if she would move me to another unit. At first, she told me they didn't have anything available, yet there were signs near the highway that said "move-in specials." Then she told me that a penthouse unit was available but she'd have to see how much the rent would cost. I got into a heated argument with her because I didn't feel like any of this was my fault, and I didn't know why I'd have to pay more in rent. I couldn't understand why they wouldn't just move me into another unit and then take their time fixing the other one. I told her that I wasn't staying there and I needed to know what she had planned on doing about this situation. She claimed that she would have to come by and check it out. So, in the meantime, I packed up my things that evening and went to a hotel. I was devastated because I feared staying in a hotel. Not only was I going to have to share hotel room walls with other guests I didn't know, but I was also going to have to get inside the elevator with them alone, too. Anything could happen within seconds. And, I didn't want to think about the fact that I'd have to walk outside from the hotel to my car in the morning to go to work. That was something I almost vowed I would never do again.

She told me they were going to fix the problem; however, when I went back to the apartment after a few days, I saw that they had cleaned up the mold and painted over it, but I could see more mold growing over the paint and this time, it was growing at a much faster pace. Not only that, I was beginning to see mold growing in my bedroom all along the walls and even more in the garage. Things were getting worse.

I spoke with the office manager and told her that I saw more mold growing over the paint. She informed me that they would check into it but that she was going on vacation and would leave the matter into one of the leasing agent's hands. I was so frustrated that the next day, Wednesday, I contacted the corporate office to speak with someone who could possibly give me some answers. I figured if I got them involved, things would move quicker. I left a message with the contact person who oversees the properties to call me and she decided to return the call on Friday around noon. She left a message letting me know that she was walking out the door leaving for the day and to also remind me that the following Monday was Memorial Day, and their office would be closed. She had no empathy at all regarding the fact that I had nowhere to stay for the next four days. I was appalled. None of this made sense to me at all. I felt violated all over again like that knife was being forced back inside my liver multiple times. How in the world could someone be so inconsiderate and cruel when I had been a tenant who never complained and always paid my rent on time? I was so upset that I just wanted to scream!

Thankfully, the last apartment complex I lived in required that I have renter's insurance and for some reason when I moved, I didn't cancel my policy, so I had coverage to stay in a hotel for a limited amount of time. That gave me some consolation, but it didn't relieve the frustration. Every emotion I had endured before thrust its way back into the forefront much stronger this time. I was angry and fearful and depressed and consumed with so much anxiety. I had only been at that apartment for five months, still trying to get used to it, and now the place I claimed as my rest haven was snatched away from me without warning. Everything was out of alignment, and I was so off balance. I felt like a cycle of violations were repeating themselves.

Each time I'd go back to the apartment, there was another story the manager would tell. She said they had to place a special order for the baseboards that lined the bathroom wall. As we waited for those to come in, more and more mold grew and each time, there was a different story. Sometimes, when I'd go back, I'd have to wear a mask because of the odor and smell. I got so frustrated that I tried to contact anybody and everybody I could to get some relief. I called the Department of Health and Hospitals, I sent certified letters to the property manager owners, and I even spoke with an attorney, but no one would relieve me of the pain I was enduring. Either I wouldn't get a response or they said there wasn't much I could do. I felt hopeless and lost. I felt like I was fighting another battle, and my opponent was laughing at me.

When they finally realized that they were going to have to treat the mold, they sent in a professional team to handle the job. In an email, I specifically told her where all the mold was growing. It had gotten so bad that it was not only growing in the bathroom, the coat closet, the bedroom, and in the living room area, but it had made its way to the kitchen pantry where I kept my food and the laundry room that sat on the other side of my kitchen. Obviously, water had traveled into some areas that I was unaware of. Then I found it growing on my furniture in my bedroom, underneath my bookshelves, and on the books and papers I had stacked on them.

Finally, she emailed me one day and told me that the apartment was ready. The team came in and cut out drywall in the areas where the water reached and took fans and dried the inside of the walls. Then they replaced it with new drywall. Because I had told her that I didn't know if I would stay there even if they fixed the issue because I didn't trust their judgment, she told me that if I did, she'd have the carpets cleaned for me.

I don't know a lot about carpentry work although my Dad had done a lot of it all his life, but I am aware of some things, and I know that when you dry a floor that has had moisture in it, you don't turn around and clean it again. Who does that? I literally thought this woman had lost her mind.

When I went back to the apartment to inspect it and make my decision, sure enough, there was still mold in some areas. I have no idea if there was some form of mis-communication between management and the professional team or if the complex just wasn't going to pay to have the extra drywall replaced or if it was their way of forcing me out. I really don't know. I just replied to her email and told her that I had inspected the apartment and there was still mold inside and I was moving. I was tired of fighting with them, and I was mentally drained. I just couldn't take it anymore.

My insurance company told me after meeting with an inspector during this whole ordeal that they could have my furniture—what I had left of it—and my clothes cleaned professionally. They also told me that they were going to seek restitution from the apartment complex and get their money back. I was glad to hear that because if they would have done what I asked, they wouldn't have had to pay out thousands of dollars for all of this. And, yes, it was thousands because I stayed in the hotel for at least a month. Not only were they spending money to have a professional team come in and replace drywall, they were going to have to deal with an insurance company and their attorneys.

Every day, after I'd get off of work or on the weekends, I'd head up to my apartment to pack up what I could take with me and dispose of things I wasn't comfortable keeping. I can remember those days, sitting inside the apartment deciphering through my things or driving to the storage I had rented to unload boxes and crying all at the same time. I had been through so much already and now the place that I considered my comfort zone had been ripped from under me again. I couldn't win for losing. I had no idea what I was going to do next. There was only one other apartment complex in the city that had attached garages, but the rent was way out of my budget. I probably could have rented a house, but would I be confident enough to stay there alone? Would it be too big? Would I be uncomfortable? Would the neighborhood be safe? Would it have enough lighting on the outside? Would it have an alarm system? All those questions filled my head, and I was just too tired to find out. I didn't want to think anymore. I didn't want to make another decision that would cause me more pain because it seemed like every decision I made in the past year did just that. I felt like life was closing in on me. I felt so defeated.

I ended up moving in with my parents who lived almost two hours away. I tried commuting to work every day—two hours to work and two hours from work. I had changed my schedule and was working ten hours per day, four days a week. It helped a little to have that extra day off, but I was still dealing with a deep stab wound that wasn't healing because of all of the stress I was under and it took the entire three days to recuperate and be ready for the next week. About three months later, I decided to resign from my position because, psychologically, I needed a break. My manager tried to get an approval to allow me to work from home three days a week, but it was denied. When that failed, I turned in my notice. If I didn't take a break, I was going to have a breakdown and I knew it. It was just too much and I couldn't function anymore. I needed some time to heal physically and mentally.

It was almost unexplainable how I felt at this point. Distraught might be a good word but I felt much worse than that. Every negative emotion that God created, I felt like I experienced it. I was so broken. I had spent the last year of my life fighting a battle that I felt like I lost. I cry just thinking about it. If I hadn't already been beaten down from becoming a victim of a violent crime, now I was homeless, jobless, broken, weak, wounded, scorned, and in distress. This time, when I hit rock bottom, suicidal thoughts came to visit me. The bad thing about it was that sometimes I felt like the advice that creeped inside my head that said to go ahead and take your life was actually the right thing to do. It seemed like the most sensible thing and I just needed a plan to carry it out. To take my life would resolve everything. I wouldn't have to worry about dealing with fear, anxiety, depression, a place to live, a job or my family worrying about me anymore. If I would just do this one thing, it would make life easier for myself and everyone else. When I thought about it and evaluated my life, it wasn't like I had accomplished anything that I was extremely proud of anyway. I wandered around for years not even having a purpose or understanding who I was. While everyone else was out living a successful, fulfilled, enjoyable life, I was just living mediocre. I was just taking up space and wasting air. I really had nothing to live for. I didn't even have an individual family of my own. And those who laughed at me and said I deserved the punishment, and talked about me and believed every rumor that was said about me, justified it even more. When I found myself going through days of deep depression like this, those thoughts became so real that it scared me. They echoed so loud in my ear pushing me and begging me to take that step. I could hear a voice so clearly saying this is the answer. I can help you. I can make it all go away. I remember one morning jumping out of bed and asking my parents to pray for me because I didn't know what else to do. I was afraid that if one more blow came my way or if I heard one more rumor about me or if another decision I made failed, I would actually carry out that plan and make it happen.

I found myself letting go of everything. I didn't want to be in control of anything. I didn't want to make another decision at all. I was so tired and exhausted. I just wanted to rest. I just wanted to inhale and exhale. I needed to be nursed back to life, refueled, and ministered to. For days, for weeks, for months, I rested. And over the course of time, I started to gain a little strength. One drip at a time, strength started to leak back into my soul until I caught on to a new perspective. But don't think for a moment that it happened all in a split second because it didn't. It took time. I had to go through the depression. I had to let go of a lot of anger, doubt, low self-esteem and many other things that were clouding my mind. I had to stop questioning God. I had to stop allowing negative thoughts to control my mind that said if I had lived a different life or made better decisions, I wouldn't be sitting in the middle of the bed contemplating taking my life. If I would have just lived my life like others and not tried to walk the narrow path, things would have been much different for me. I would have been happier and successful like everyone else. Sometimes I'd go back and forth, and up and down with my feelings. One minute I'm doing good and the next was like a bomb shell ready to drop. That's kind of how it is when you're deeply depressed and having thoughts of suicide. One minute you're fine, laughing and talking, and the next minute you want to take your life.

I wrestled for so long that sometimes, I wondered if I could beat this thing and come out on top. I was physically and mentally tired. Life had literally grabbed me by the throat and was choking me slowly. It was almost as if I stopped breathing but somehow in the midst of it all I continued to inhale and exhale. With the little air that I could salvage, I wondered if I would one day be the last man standing in all of this.

CHAPTER 22

Lessons Learned

∽

For I will restore health unto thee,
and I will heal thee of thy wounds,
saith the Lord. (Jeremiah 30:17)

I LOOK AT PICTURES OF myself before my incident occurred and think about how free I was, smiling and posing without a care in the world. If someone would have told me that I was going to face such a treacherous storm, I don't think I would have believed in myself enough to have the strength to conquer the adversity. But, I have made it so far. It is hard and every day isn't always easy, but I am here. Sometimes, I have to sternly remind myself that I am going to get through this somehow. Sometimes, it is still a fight.

Does it mean that I am not a winner because I still stumble and struggle? No. It means that I am human, but I have this phenomenal relationship with an unbelievably strong God who loves me and helps me triumph every single day. I don't live because of my own strength, but it is God's strength that lives inside of me that keeps me going. Every day I fight to stay alive. I go before the thrown of grace asking for strength to make it. See, it isn't a one-time thing. You just don't get over it and move on. It is a process where you wake up every morning and fight to live and before going to bed at night, you reflect on the fact that you conquered that day. And, if it doesn't go so well and you incur some dark moments, you know that you have yet another chance to make it better tomorrow because God's mercies are new every single morning (Lamentations 3:22-23). He is faithful to see us through and be there with us every step of the way.

I have learned so many lessons in this storm and so much about myself. First, I had to come to terms with the fact that God is sovereign and that He allowed this to happen to me. Yes, He allowed it. It took some time for me to accept that because for so long I questioned Him. How could a God who calls me His daughter and promises to protect me allow me to go through such a brutal attack? But He needed me to experience the pain, violence, depression and alot emotions because He has a plan to use me for a specific purpose in some way. We may not always understand what God is doing in our lives, but we have to trust Him whole heartedly. At one point, I had to lay down my anger and frustration towards Him, ask Him to forgive me, and learn how to trust. I had to come to the conclusion that this incident had nothing to do with any decisions

I made or did not make, or where I lived or my financial status. It was just my season to endure a storm like this. Ecclesiastes 3:1 says "To everything there is a season, and a time to every purpose under the heaven." It was my season to weep and mourn, and for a part of me to die, and there was nothing I could have done to change that. And when I felt like He had walked away from me, He was there all the time and He never left me. It was my faith that was weak. I focused more on my storm rather than looking to Him. Even when I displayed anger and bitterness, He still loved me and cared for me. Every single time I got upset, He forgave me and had mercy on me. Through this process, I was able to experience His unconditional love and peace in a way that I had never before. Now my faith has been restored in Him. I have confidence and believe that He has my best interest at heart for every situation and in all things. No matter what, He will never leave me or forsake me, and He will forever protect and cover me. I can trust and believe in that.

Second, I've learned that I am a lot stronger and have more courage than I ever imagined. God's strength was made perfect in my weakness (II Corinthians 12:9). There was no way that I was able to pull through any of this without His help. I could not have done this alone. He had more faith in me and believed in me when I didn't believe in myself. When I cried out to Him and said I couldn't do this anymore, He stood back in silence on purpose be-cause He wanted me to exercise my own faith in Him and exercise my own muscles in this fight to gain strength. I thought that being strong is when you stand up and fight in the face of your adversary but I've learned that being strong is when you do nothing at all. It is when you allow God to fight your battles for you. It is having the courage to lay down your weapon and allow God to take control.

Third, I've learned that I am a different person now. It took some time but I had to finally realize that a part of me died that day. After desperately searching through therapy and the support group and even in my own way to fix my problems and get my old life back, I realized that the old me wasn't coming back. And no matter how hard I tried, I had to let her go. She no longer existed and I had to come to terms with that. I had to learn how to live without her. I had to learn how to make the best of my life where I was. I had to find freedom and happiness in the new me. I couldn't spend the rest of my life searching for a dead soul. It would profit me absolutely nothing. But now I know who I am. I am a survivor, a fighter, courageous, and strong and not a victim. I plant seeds of hope and healing in the lives of others. I possess a passion I didn't have before. I view life differently. I see hurting people in a different way. Every time I hear of a tragedy of someone becoming a victim, I pray for them because I know what it is like and I know what they are about to face. I often ask God to give them the courage to survive and give them hope to believe that things will get better, and to protect their mind, their thoughts and cover them with His love.

One day, I remember sitting and talking with my dad. I was upset and crying and really frustrated because this happened to me. I was so tired of my life being out of alignment and I just wanted things to fall back into place. I wanted my life to flow again. I wanted to be happy and have joy and peace. I wanted to wake up in the mornings with purpose and drive. I wanted to live again. And I remember my dad quoting this scripture to me. Hebrews 10:9 that says "God takes away the first to establish the second" meaning all of those negative things that have attached themselves to us and branded us during our childhood, teenage years and adulthood that distracts us from completely following the will of God for our lives, He removes. It is like a rebirth. He starts all over again with us. And sometimes, He'll allow a storm to come into our lives to start that process. Whether it's insecurities, fear, doubt, or low self-esteem, He has to take it away to establish who He really designed for us to be so that we can fulfill His purpose in our lives.

Thinking about that, I can remember so many times dealing with fear. Even when I was a child, fear always played a huge role in my life. I can still remember those times when I was too afraid to stand up and speak in front of an audience, or give my honest heartfelt opinion about something afraid someone would disagree. Or, those times when I would sing and my hands would tremble. When God gave me instructions to do something, I was too afraid to step out concerned about what others would say or if I had the resources to complete the task. Maybe that is why fear played such a tedious role in my life during this storm. Maybe God allowed me to deal with it on a deeper level to experience and recognize its behavior. Perhaps I needed to understand that fear is powerful only if I allow it to be.

I won't say that I have mastered fear but I am learning to live life and do things even if I am afraid. Just like I walked out that front door after being locked up for seven days, I did it afraid. So whether I am a little nervous while speaking before a large audience, traveling alone or even conquering a simple task as going to the movies alone, I'm learning to not allow fear to control me. Even with it riding on my shoulders, I am learning that the task doesn't have to be aborted just because I am afraid. It doesn't matter how I feel, whether I am afraid or not, what matters is that I step out and start. That is the key.

So as I continue to lean on God for strength, I hope that one day the very essence of fear would be at such a distance that I won't think twice about it. But for now, I'll just keep healing, hoping and believing that things will get better as each day goes by.

CHAPTER 23

Dear Fear

Dear Fear,

Before I was assaulted, I always related you to just a minor force that tried to stop someone from speaking in front of a crowd or enslaving someone to never get over the fear of heights. But, I have found out that you are much more than that. I now realize that you truly are a spirit, a force that would like to control me and enslave me, to isolate me from being free.

I sit here and think about my life and remember those times I didn't really know you. I allowed you to control me. I was your slave and you were my master. There were times when I was too afraid to speak up, too afraid to be that sold-out child for God, too afraid to open up my heart to another, too afraid to step out, too afraid to live, too afraid to love myself. I declare today that I will never allow you to control me again. This experience with you has completely changed my life. You really don't know what you have done for me. You think that you have caused me damage but actually, you have really set me free. Now I will go out into the world with a different attitude. With an attitude that I will serve God and Him only—that I won't worry about what others think of me, that I am valuable and I deserve everything that comes my way.

I am writing you this letter because I want you to know where we stand. I want you to know that we will never have a relationship nor will we ever be friends. Although I am still taking baby steps and jumping over hurdles one day at a time, I want you to know that with God's help, I am gaining back control of my life. I may not be where I used to be, but I'll get there. I'll be such a threat to you. I'll tell everyone everywhere I go about your tactics and your ways; they will know who you are. And, when you come knocking at their door, they'll recognize you and send you on your way.

Blog Post: "Dear Fear"

Made in the USA
Columbia, SC
02 January 2018